LIVING WITH THE REALITY OF
DISSOCIATIVE IDENTITY DISORDER

LIVING WITH THE REALITY OF DISSOCIATIVE IDENTITY DISORDER
Campaigning Voices

Edited by
Lady Xenia Bowlby
and Deborah Briggs

KARNAC

First published in 2014 by
Karnac Books Ltd
118 Finchley Road
London NW3 5HT

British Library Cataloguing in Publication Data

A C.I.P. for this book is available from the British Library

ISBN-13: 978-1-78220-134-2

Typeset by V Publishing Solutions Pvt Ltd., Chennai, India

Printed in Great Britain

www.karnacbooks.com

CONTENTS

ACKNOWLEDGEMENTS   vii

ABOUT THE EDITORS AND CONTRIBUTORS   ix

FOREWORD   xiii
by Xenia Bowlby

CHAPTER ONE
Introduction   1
Pat Frankish

CHAPTER TWO
The art of Kim Noble   5
Kim Noble

CHAPTER THREE
Spiritual aspects of DID   13
Nicky Robertson

CHAPTER FOUR
Reading, writing, and reeling   23
Oriel Winslow

CHAPTER FIVE
The role of friends in recovery   35
Carolyn Bramhall and Deborah Briggs

CHAPTER SIX
Satanic Ritual Abuse (the painful truth)   49
Paula Bennett

CHAPTER SEVEN
Personal and societal denial   57
Carolyn Spring

CHAPTER EIGHT
Living with DID   67
Carol Broad

CHAPTER NINE
Back to normal? Surviving life with dissociation   81
Rob Spring

CHAPTER TEN
Living well is the best revenge   93
Sue Bridger

CHAPTER ELEVEN
Medical aspects of recognising complex dissociative disorders   105
Ruth Cureton

CHAPTER TWELVE
How far have we come?   123
Orit Badouk Epstein

INDEX   129

ACKNOWLEDGEMENTS

Thanks are due to Valerie Sinason and Pat Frankish for their help with the preparation of this book.

Dr Pat Frankish was the first chair of Paracelsus (dedicated to the needs of people with DID) and recently retired from that role. Dr Valerie Sinason has established the Clinic for Dissociative Studies (CDS) and works tirelessly for people with DID.

The campaign for better recognition of DID, and help for those affected, began in 2011 and will continue until the aims are achieved.

ABOUT THE EDITORS AND CONTRIBUTORS

Paula Bennett is in her early 50s and has been writing and speaking about her abuse to professional groups and survivor groups in the last few years. She made the decision to be more public and was on the front page of the *Sunday Express* in January 2013 speaking of ritual abuse by Jimmy Savile as well as reporting him to the police. She is currently working on further autobiographical chapters and adding to the training of professionals in the field of ritual abuse, mind control, and dissociation.

Xenia Bowlby is the daughter-in-law of John Bowlby, whose research has given so much to our understanding of complex personalities. She supports her husband Richard to continue the work and has been active in the development of the Paracelsus Trust.

Carolyn Bramhall is founder and director of Heart for Truth, an organisation which equips churches and communities to effectively lead the most hurting and emotionally damaged into health. Her book *Am I A Good Girl Yet?* tells the story of her personal journey out of DID and other effects of Satanic ritual abuse. A counsellor and pastoral consultant, she has thirty years' experience working with troubled people in a variety of contexts in Britain and America, particularly within the framework of the Christian church. She holds diplomas in theology, Christian work, and counselling, is married to John, an Anglican clergyman, and has two grown-up children.

Sue Bridger has spent many years preparing a toolkit for therapists and people with a diagnosis of DID.

Deborah Briggs is chair of the Paracelsus Trust. She has worked as a therapist for a decade and specialises in trauma and sexual abuse. Her training is integrative, including relational, sensorimotor, and psychodynamic psychotherapy. Deborah has friends with DID, some of whom are fellow therapists or trainers.

Carol Broad is a survivor of sexual abuse and incest, officially diagnosed with DID in 2008 after many years in the wilderness of the mental health system. Carol views herself as a survivor of the NHS, having spent nearly four years as an in-patient in various hospitals. An expert by experience she speaks at conferences and training events across the UK and internationally about dissociative disorders and mental health issues. She is actively involved in raising awareness of mental health and challenging stigma and discrimination. A member of her local Pentecostal church, her faith keeps her strong.

Dr Ruth Cureton (B Med Sci, BM BS) is married with three grown-up children. Ruth worked as a GP for over 20 years around her family commitments before taking early retirement. Since 2005 she has been involved in the charitable sector and now works as development manager for Willows Counselling Service, Swindon; trustee and membership secretary of the Trauma and Abuse Group (TAG); trustee of First Person Plural (FPP); and is a member of the UK Research Group of the European Society for Trauma and Dissociation (ESTD).

Orit Badouk Epstein is an attachment-based psychoanalytic psychotherapist (UKCP registered) and a supervisor working in private practice. She works relationally with all client groups and has a particular interest in and passion for working with people who have experienced extreme abuse and trauma displaying symptoms of dissociation. Orit is a trustee for the Clinic for Dissociative Studies. She is co-author of

Ritual Abuse and Mind Control: the Manipulation of Attachment Needs (Karnac, 2011), regularly writes articles and film and book reviews, and is on the editorial boards for the journal *Attachment* and the European Society for Trauma and Dissociation newsletter.

Dr Pat Frankish is a consultant clinical psychologist and disability psychotherapist specialising in providing services for people with complex needs, including DID. She is a past president of the British Psychological Society, and the first chair of the Paracelsus Trust and the Institute of Psychotherapy and Disability. She runs her own group of companies with her daughter, who is also a disability psychotherapist. These companies provide direct support services, individual therapy, therapeutic environments, and training within the field of complex needs.

Kim Noble is a mother, artist, and author and happens to have DID. Her autobiography *All of me* was published by Piatkus in 2011 and has been translated into several languages. She has had more than sixty solo and group exhibitions throughout the UK, Europe and the USA, and her work can be found in many galleries and collections. She has been filmed and interviewed for television and radio shows worldwide including Japan, Australia, and the USA. She appeared on the Oprah Winfrey closing show in 2010 and *This Morning* with Philip Schofield and Holly Willoughby in 2012.

Nicky Robertson is 57 years old, is married to a vicar, and has three grown-up children. She was diagnosed with severe DID, post traumatic stress disorder, and depression some years ago. From her experience with the church she has addressed the spiritual aspects of the condition.

Carolyn Spring is a freelance writer and has DID as a result of organised abuse in childhood. After studying at Cambridge university, she worked for a number of years in children's social care supporting at-risk families and caring for children who had suffered abuse and neglect. She also has a background in business, with experience in marketing, website design, IT and adult training. Carolyn is a director of TASC (Trauma and Abuse Support Centre), a web-based resource for adult survivors of child sexual abuse. Alongside her husband Rob she is a director of PODS (Positive Outcomes for Dissociative Survivors) where she has specific responsibility for writing and delivering training, as well as strategic oversight of the project. She is also chair of START (Survivors Trauma and Abuse Recovery Trust), a charity formed in 2011 to support work in trauma and abuse recovery. Carolyn is in the process of completing her first book, is a former editor of *Interact*, the journal of TAG (Trauma and Abuse Group), and is editor of *Multiple Parts*, the magazine of PODS. She is in great demand as a conference speaker and freelance trainer, and speaks throughout the UK on her experiences of trauma, abuse, and dissociation.

Rob Spring has a degree in biology and a postgraduate certificate of education from Swansea university; he worked as a secondary school teacher for ten years, including four years as head of department at a private school. He then moved briefly into adult education and training on a self-employed basis before working alongside Carolyn in children's social care for a number of years, looking after neglected and abused children. Rob is a director of PODS with responsibility for the helpline and the provision of one-to-one support. Alongside Carolyn he delivers training for PODS to survivors and their lay or professional supporters. He is also undertaking counselling training.

Oriel Winslow is a trustee and secretary of First Person Plural, a national survivor-led charity working with DID. Oriel is committed to raising awareness about the existence and reality of DID. Prior to being formally diagnosed with DID in 2008, Oriel studied English literature at Royal Holloway, and began an MA in contemporary poetry. However, a breakdown in 2007 led to having to interrupt her studies and come to terms with her diagnosis and childhood trauma. One of the reasons she believes in the vital importance of educating people about DID is that she feels it was only post-diagnosis that she could begin to genuinely make informed choices about her life, and manage her system.

FOREWORD

Everyone should read this collection of extraordinary and very moving—but never self-pitying—writings. We need to understand the shattering effect of trauma: how it splinters the mind and damages the body—whether directly or psychosomatically—and how it can break the spirit and assault the soul. These chapters were first presented at a Campaign Day for survivors on 12th March 2011.

Government, law enforcement, the justice system, and all of us who make up "society" need to recognise that terrible abuse happens, and that it is often organised and always hidden. The perpetrators are always powerful—privately or publicly—and their targets are always the most vulnerable people, and this makes it particularly difficult for us to be brave enough to address the problem.

It is a privilege to read the accounts of these amazing survivors who have had the courage to share their journeys. They describe their confusion and self-doubt and, sometimes, their denial of the trauma that they experienced; and how the lack of understanding of their situation, the ignorance of Dissociative Identity Disorder (DID) as a possible diagnosis, and the difficulty in finding therapeutic help, have all impeded their progress from great distress and dissociation to greater self-knowledge and a truly humbling optimism about the future.

Xenia Bowlby

CHAPTER ONE

Introduction

Pat Frankish

This book aims to bring together the threads that make up the campaign for people with Dissociative Identity Disorder (DID). The many threads reflect the multiplicity of the condition and this will become apparent as you read on. Weaving the threads together should be healing and that is one of the aims of the campaign. The multiplicity is both rich and confusing. Supporting people with DID can be exhausting. Living with it is both confusing and exhausting. DID is a survival mechanism and reflects the strength of the basic psyche to survive experiences that would drive some to psychosis.

The Clinic for Dissociative Studies (CDS) has taken a lead in the diagnosis and treatment of people with DID. Valerie Sinason has been a major contributor to the sharing of knowledge and raising the profile of this disabling condition. She has also been influential in highlighting ritual abuse as one of the main causes. This situation has led to many attacks from people who try to conceal their identity and role in the horrific abuse that people with DID report. Valerie, in particular, who has been willing to be named and to speak out, has been attacked in the press and on the internet. She continues to be brave and withstand these attacks, and is well supported by her colleagues to do this. The Bowlby Centre, looking at attachment and how this has been

1

damaged in people with DID, offers further interventions. These two organisations have pioneered the therapeutic work with people with DID. Many people with DID, including some of the contributors to this book, have endured life without the benefit of formal therapy directed at the condition. They have found their way through the maze and survived. Their work is testament to their courage and strength.

A recent article in the *Observer* (December 2011) paints a distorted picture of the condition and the causes, leaving ordinary readers confused and perhaps thinking we are all mentally deranged. It is hard to believe that people will harm their own children the way they do, but that is not sufficient reason to fail to believe the real-life experience of some very brave and distressed people. It is inevitable that this book will involve many references to ritual abuse, but it is primarily about survival and living with the consequences of life experiences that attempt to destroy the self. Of course, it is the core identity that is attacked in ritual abuse, as this ensures that the person on the receiving end can often be discredited as an unreliable witness.

My own role has been in the development, registration, and running of the Paracelsus Trust. This is a registered charity, with the objective of supporting the people who attend the clinic for things that are not funded from their care package. The initial benefactors were Pearl King and Tina Carlile. Sadly Tina is no longer with us but she left a bequest in her will to support the charity. The trust has engaged in some fundraising but relies primarily on legacies. It has been, and is, within the remit of the trust to support the campaign and we were pleased to be able to provide some financial support for the campaign meetings in March 2010 as well as for people attending, to ensure that the days were a success.

The original Paracelsus was an early advocate of medical interventions, with a wide approach to what might work. He was often rejected for his ideas and spent much of his time wandering around the world looking for acceptance. He was a brilliant man already very capable by the age of sixteen. He died in 1541 after a short illness, with some admirers of his skill and knowledge of alchemy, and others who rejected him outright. There are so many similarities for people with DID and those who work for them that it seemed a good name for the trust. He was a leader in his field and he persevered even after rejection. No doubt this sounds familiar to many people reading this book. Paracelsus is another thread in the weave.

Amelia Roberts was funded by the clinic and the trust to carry out the administration of the campaign days, and we thank her for this. The first day was for survivors and their therapists. The second day was for parliamentarians and commissioners of services. Attendance at both was significant and a considerable amount of information was shared. We are optimistic that more developments will follow and that, in time, people with DID will receive the services they need, and ritual abuse will be brought into the open and stopped.

The Paracelsus Trust is independent of any of the organisations that are represented in the campaign, and this independence allows the trustees to help without creating schisms in, or between, the activist groups. Everyone who contributes is valued and necessary, but it is interesting to note that there are so many different organisations, making it look like a replica of DID. It would be good to see everyone come together in an integrated way and perhaps Paracelsus can help with this. I have retired from the chair of the trust but continue as a trustee and it would be a delight for me to hear that the separate groups were able to combine their energies for the benefit of all.

My studies over the years have taken me into systems and what makes organisations function in the way they do. Individuals in organisations sometimes can't recognise what happens when it is far removed from their own position. Systems reflect the pressures that come from inside as has been well documented by Obholzer et al. (1994). There is a system within the person and a system that the person lives within. The total system is the whole of society, but people exist within microsystems, sometimes family, sometimes support services and, of course, for people with DID, often within a cult. The power of systems should not be underestimated. Ritualised abuse can produce systems with internal destructive systems as well as the fractured personality that enables power to be retained by the abusers. The systems within systems are confusing and exhausting for the individual affected and for those who support them. It is common for people with DID to refer to their body and their internal system as separate entities, making statements like "the body's age is ..." and "within my system there are many alters, all with their own role". It is a joy to meet people with DID who have found a way to live a good life and some of them have written chapters in this book.

The internal system of someone with DID is fragmented and only has some communication lines on the inside. A communication book, where each member of the system can write, enables them to find out who is there, but no one has a picture of everyone who is there, their individual roles, or a shared history. It falls to the therapist or other supporters to help to establish a full history, from the information provided by each of the alters, and to try to enable the present host or group to accept this and live with it. There is grief over the loss of alters who disappear, although it must be at least possible, and maybe likely, that the ones who disappear have served their purpose in keeping the body alive and the mind stable. Kim Noble, in her book *All of Me* (2011) and her chapter here, shows us how the different people who share her body can communicate with each other and the world through art. Each of her personalities has an individual painting style, making them identifiable and distinct from each other.

People with DID are survivors. They have endured horrific experiences. The way that their psyche has fractured has allowed them to survive physically and not be killed or kill themselves. The horror of their childhood has been managed through the process of splitting off so that most have no memory of what happened. Those who do suffer begin to be able to talk about it, but this can be restricted to the times that they are aware of being "out". Coping strategies become very complex and intricate, with switching happening to ensure the safety of the whole body. These themes are developed in this book.

The chapters are all written by survivors until the last one where Orit Badouk Epstein offers a brief summary and some closing thoughts on the processes involved in the campaign meeting and the writing of the book, which in itself has been a process of bringing together diverse information. Each chapter has an internal coherence, recognising that the authors have reached a level of integration in their survival journey. We hope that together they provide a link to the book and the campaign, enabling all of us to continue in the endeavour to bring these very real issues into a wider consciousness in the public arena.

References

Noble, K. (2011). *All of Me*. London: Piatkus.
Obholzer, A., & Roberts, V. Z. (2005). *The Unconscious at Work: Individual and Organizational Stress in the Human Services* (2nd edn). Abingdon: Routledge.

CHAPTER TWO

The art of Kim Noble

Kim Noble

From the age of fourteen we had been in and out of hospital with several different diagnoses like anorexia, bulimia, psychosis, depression, post-traumatic stress, alcoholism, and schizophrenia. No one understood about DID then. Now I understand that twenty main alters and many fragments share my body. Many of them have trouble accepting the idea that they share a body even though they have been told. I do understand how hard it is for them and for the rest of the population to make sense of DID as I had the same problem when I was diagnosed in 1995. I blamed my memory problems on too much drinking. I was only drinking one or two glasses of wine but I seemed to always have a glass in my hand. I thought I must be an alcoholic. If you are sharing a body with other alters then you also share time so my time can be very much limited.

I am often asked, "What does it feel like to have DID?" The strange thing is that each of us is a person in our own right, no different from anyone else, so it is normal for us. It is how we have always been.

The main problem for me now is the lost time or lack of memory as we are not co-conscious when another personality is in control of the body. To explain this to someone who has not experienced DID is hard but I think it is a similar experience to sleep walking. You can be told that you walked downstairs, ate some cake, and went back to bed. Yet you have no memory of it, just the evidence of the missing cake. I can get up in the morning, find a new painting in the studio, and I have no memory of doing it. The important point is that another personality painted it so I wouldn't have their memory.

I started painting seven years ago. It began because a support worker came round who was training to be an art therapist. She said while we were chatting we could do some painting. I said I could not paint and we had no paints. She found some wallpaper and some of my daughter's paints and we were able to paint on the back of it. Seven of us took part in the next few months. This took place in my dining room on the table. But the paint went everywhere so we turned the small bedroom into a studio.

Since then, another seven have found enjoyment and a way of communicating and expressing themselves through their art. We all have our own distinctive style and many of them are unaware they share a body. However, all are informed about our exhibitions. Judy does ask why she has to share her exhibitions with Kim Noble and not have a solo exhibition under her own name. She knows about DID but does not think she has it. That way, the personalities who do not understand they have DID are still prepared.

I remember our first exhibition in London and the feeling of closeness, warmth, and pride I felt as I looked around the gallery. It helped me realise for the first time that this was the nearest I was ever going to get to meeting my alters. Being untrained artists our work comes from our heart and not our head. Every painting exhibited was part of us on the wall, communicating a message, expressing an emotion, and telling a story. I could see for once at least fourteen of us were on the same page, heading down the same road, having an activity that we enjoyed.

After seeing the huge amount of space our paintings take up in exhibitions we feel the contrast with our space at home. Our studio is a small room and has trouble housing fourteen artists. However, we manage to share the space and respect one another's work. Quite often I see unfinished canvasses lined up in the hall. In order to have room to paint, whoever is there has to take others' work out of the studio as there isn't the room for them to paint otherwise. The paintings are lined up like people waiting in a queue.

I have no memory at all between the personalities and scientific research has confirmed this. When I come back, by which I mean take control of the body, I don't always know who's been around. The best way to tell is to look at what painting is out at the time. Since we started the artwork, there's actually been a lot more control in my life. If they're painting, they're achieving something, and when they don't, they get very restless.

I can tell you a little about the fourteen artists and their paintings but my words haven't come from them, it is my interpretation of their works and what they have told family, friends, and our therapist.

The artist personalities

Abi likes to paints lone figures—her paintings portray loneliness and emptiness; she often leaves a lot of blank canvas with just a lone figure in the corner.

The thinking man.

Anon is called Anon as we don't know her name. She usually paints in the early hours of the morning so nobody is there to ask her name. Her work is of a mystic nature. Her technique is extremely unusual with the paint poured directly onto the canvas and limited use of a palette knife.

Edge of the circle.

Bonny is one of the few alters who accept DID. She was the main carer of our daughter. Aimee, our daughter, was removed at birth by social services who felt we would never be able to bring her up. After a six-month fight in court Aimee was returned and we have had her with us ever since. She is now a beautiful, intelligent, caring, happy, stable 15-year-old (that's my opinion!). After the struggles with social services Bonny felt unable to cope and didn't come out as much. Bonny's paintings are usually bright and contain robotic figures or stick-like people.

Dawn is the personality who gave birth to Aimee, even though we would have all loved to have been there, so she was Aimee's birth mother. She often uses a sponge to apply the paint onto the canvas, often using poetry within the painting.

Longing rose.

Judy is a 15-year-old bulimic teenager who sees herself as overweight. She likes to paint with a palette knife and she is one of my favourite artists. There often seems to be a hidden, subtle meaning in her work.

Karen is probably the artist I know least about other than that all her paintings are painted with a toothbrush (not the one I use!).

Ken is a young gay guy. He was the last of us to start painting and has been painting for three years. He wanted to paint a train but got frustrated with not being able to paint it so he slapped it onto the wall and turned it round and this is how he now does all his paintings. He liked the texture and the fresh mixed colours when the canvas was pulled off the wall.

Key's paintings are full of little pictures and symbols. She uses the Kabbalah and Hebrew words and letters. I have no knowledge of the Kabbalah or Hebrew and I am not sure where she obtained her knowledge.

Mimi has only painted three paintings with two more ongoing. Hers take longest—her work can take three years. Her pictures are very childlike and bright and bold. Aimee asked her what her name was and she said "Me! Me!" and we don't know whether she was repeating the word Me or saying Mimi!

Missy MJ does not talk much. Missy will only use three colours: red, black, and white. She throws the paint onto the canvas with more landing on the floor than the painting, even ending up on the walls and window. She either paints with fierce energy or will stand for ages dripping the paint onto the canvas. When handed another colour by our daughter Missy refused to use it. Aimee, when young, particularly enjoyed being in the studio with Missy as she would be covered in paint when finished!

Patricia. That's me and my work. I find myself the most boring of the artists—usually calm seascapes. I am now the main personality who looks after Aimee and does all the boring chores of running the house.

Ria's paintings are of child abuse. She uses bright colours and has told people that this is deliberate. She wants the paintings to be seen so that people have to take a look at them. If they are so bright, they are there and can't be missed, unlike child abuse where people don't believe, don't want to believe, or just turn away. They depict dissociation too. When I first saw her paint on canvas, not just on wallpaper, it was a colour that looked dirty and when I picked it up I felt my hand would get dirty. I got a cloth to hold it, not because the paint was wet but because I felt my hands would get dirty from holding the picture. It was not her most graphic but it was so powerful.

Round the corner.

Salome is a committed and serious Catholic and a private person who does not want her paintings publicly described or exhibited.

Suzy paints a picture on canvas and when finished scribbles over it. She has painted several pictures of a mother and baby. After months of repeating the theme, Suzy painted a picture that had a golden curtain over it. When I took a look there was the same painting background as in all the mother and baby paintings but the baby was missing. After that she has never repeated the same painting again but moved on to copy pictures of celebrities. The next stage of her painting was to use her imagination and now there is more originality to her painting.

Meet the gingers.

I sign all the painting with a symbol of the body name, Kim. This I feel to be the best way as the personalities do not sign their own paintings. I have left a message in the studio asking them to but they haven't taken any notice. They are just interested in the painting; not so much signing, titles, or exhibiting.

I had never intended to make my DID public. However, when different art galleries told me they liked my work but wanted me to come back when my style was settled and consistent I realised there was no other way forward. I am glad other people feel hope that someone with DID can be an artist, author, and mother, and that is where my own hopes reside.

CHAPTER THREE

Spiritual aspects of DID

Nicky Robertson

I am 57 years old, married to a vicar, and have three grown-up children. Five years ago I was diagnosed with severe dissociative identity disorder, post traumatic stress disorder, and depression.

After two years of battling for an assessment and a further two years of battling for funding, I have had three years of specialist therapy funded by the NHS. In that time I have been able to begin to face the trauma of the past, and in particular of the ritual abuse I suffered. To date I have around twenty-one known person parts or identities, and a lot of therapy so far has revolved around accepting those different parts, recognising how and why they were created, and acknowledging the roles that they took in helping me to survive.

A significant part of the journey through therapy for us has also been wrestling with the spiritual aspects of abuse. This has meant facing the effects that satanic rituals had on the ability to hold a faith of any kind in adulthood. But it has also meant wrestling with each internal person's sense of spiritual identity. There is, I think, a generally held belief that we are made up of body, mind, and soul or spirit. But while much has been written about the effects of trauma and abuse on the body and mind, I have found very little consideration given to the effects of abuse on the spirit.

Only in Christian circles have I found even the remotest references to spiritual trauma. I was struck many years ago by a comment in a book about child abuse and the church. The author claimed that abuse was tantamount to "murder of the soul". Was this an accurate comment or an exaggeration? Certainly huge damage is done to us as survivors emotionally. But what is also damaged is our concept of self and of self-worth, of who we are, and where we fit in. This surely goes deeper than just the emotions. The question of who we are plumbs the very depths of our souls. This becomes more complex for anyone who develops dissociative identity disorder as a result of intolerable trauma. There is not just one self to try to understand but several internal identities.

In most, if not all, societies there is recognition of what that society considers right and wrong, of good and evil. Although there is great debate about moral standards in today's society, and what is and is not acceptable, there is a strong belief in fundamental values of what is right and wrong. Murder, lying, and stealing are just a few of the actions that are considered wrong or even evil.

Those of us who are survivors of severe abuse and trauma have perhaps a greater awareness than most of man's potential for great evil. It is not as hard perhaps for us to grasp that mankind is capable of great depths of depravity. But what of the concept of good in mankind? While people unaffected by trauma and abuse may have firmly held beliefs in man's goodness, is that ability to trust and believe in any goodness potentially "murdered" by severe abuse?

Severe attachment issues, lack of trust, fear of people generally and men especially, can be just some of the results of awful damage in childhood. All humans search for acceptance, love, and secure attachment. Attachment theory acknowledges the need in us all to attach securely as infants to a safe caregiver. When such care is not available because the caregiver can't or won't give it, then attachment issues develop and continue into adulthood, with chaotic or insecure attachment patterns developing. The ability to believe we are loved or loveable, or even acceptable, can be badly damaged. But does this damage go deeper than just the unfulfilled need for a safe parent or caregiver? And in our awareness of evil, where does our longing for good, for acceptance, for self-worth, for love, come from?

I would like to share my personal experience in wrestling with these questions.

I knew as a child that there had to be good in the world; and more than that, a god. I do not know why I believed that or where I got it. It was certainly not from my parents, who were the main perpetrators of the abuse I went through. As satanists their belief system centred on gaining power over others. This was not achieved by what society might term as good. Perhaps my beliefs were a reaction to the evil around me that made up my formative years.

I did have glimpses of different attitudes, particularly from a kind uncle who had bipolar disorder. I loved him so much as a child. In his high states he was enormous fun to be with, and when low would just disappear for a while. I could identify with that. He had a gentle nature and was particularly caring towards others, always ready to help anyone in need where he could. Although he had no faith in God, he had a belief in being good and generous wherever possible. He was not around enough to become a significant attachment figure but he taught me, I think, that there was the possibility of a different way of being to that which I experienced from my parents.

I also had a deep love of nature and the privilege of growing up on the edge of the Peak District. This meant I had somewhere to escape alone in beautiful surroundings whenever I could. The Bible does say that creation itself cries out in testimony to a creator God. Certainly there was, and is, in me a continued awe at the beauty of creation. To me it made sense that there had to be a creator. As I grew up and was trained more rigorously by the group my parents belonged to, torture and mind control played havoc with these beliefs. As I dissociated more and more to survive, there was in effect a murdering of the soul.

By the time I was a teenager deep depression had set in. I had little or no sense of self-worth and found it difficult to believe anyone would accept me. I was low enough to consider taking my own life at the age of seventeen. I still have the note that I wrote then. It is written as a dialogue with the imagined reader, about the rights or wrongs of suicide. In it I wrestled with whether there really was a god who would judge trying to take my own life, or if it was in fact a brave action to escape "the concentration camp" of earth. Strong words from a very troubled soul.

Around that time I got to know a girl in my art class at school, who had recently become a Christian. At first I was deeply suspicious of her; for a start she was better than me at art, and I hated her for that! But gradually, listening to her conversations with others, I began to hear about a loving, caring god. A god who had come down in the human form of his son to die as a sacrifice, paying in our place for all the wrong we had done and all that separated us from him. Now sacrifice was something I understood. I had seen enough of it in the satanic group, where sacrifice of pure, innocent babies and children was routine to gain approval and power. There had even been occasions where I'd had to choose who might be punished, raped, or die in my place. But God taking the punishment himself for me, because he loves me?! Nothing in my upbringing allowed for any understanding of forgiveness, or acceptance, or of how to deal with the awful wrongs I had been through and taken part in.

At this point all I knew was that I needed so much this love and acceptance, and to be free of the awful guilt and shame I felt. I could scarcely believe that it was possible to be loved, or that I was worth anything, but I chose to accept all that Christ had done and commit my life to him. Even just taking the step of making a choice for me was massive; in the world I grew up in this would never have been allowed. But in making that choice something shifted dramatically. In the Bible it says: "For he has rescued us from the kingdom of darkness and brought us into the kingdom of his dear Son, who purchased our freedom and forgave our sins" (Colossians 1:13).

I wish I could say it was easy to make that choice and that my parents accepted my new found beliefs but of course they did not. I suffered terrible punishment at the hands of the group, and many attempts were made to make sure I conformed again and never spoke out. For many years, at one level, they succeeded but something had radically changed inside and a part of me knew I would never be able to be completely drawn back again into that darkness. I knew that the Bible verse I clung to was true, and somehow I had indeed been rescued, even if at the time I did not know entirely from what, as dissociation meant I had no conscious memories of the awful abuse I had endured. The depression and sense of "dis ease" continued. I had nightmares and lost time, and had a sense of something awful and black and huge within, like a cancerous growth.

Some years later I suffered my first breakdown while teaching, and over the next years began to unravel, and the many person parts that went up to make me started to dare to speak and to share their trauma. I went through years of misdiagnosis and inappropriate treatment, before a final diagnosis of severe DID.

As I said earlier, I have around twenty-one different parts, and in my journey through therapy I have discovered something I think important and profound. Each one of them has their own experience of life, and wrestle with who they are, what they were, who they might be now. Each one of them has had to make their own spiritual journey. They, as I have done and continue to do, have had to wrestle with the big issues of good and evil, and the place of forgiveness.

Just because I am a Christian does not mean they share my values or beliefs. But each has needed the space to find they actually have the choice to face those questions for themselves. Choice is something we were never given by the group; not real choices that were not double binds, designed to break our spirit even more. Each part as they have emerged has wrestled with whether it is possible to make choices for themselves and not be punished as a result. As they have come through the process of therapy, of recognising that it is "now, not then", and that the group who harmed them is not around any more to impose their rules, or to force them into the roles they were created for, then questions have arisen. If they are not needed in the same ways any more, then what is their role now? Who are they? And then there are the deep questions we all face about the meaning of life and whether there is a God.

One example is Jane, my internal seventeen-year-old who was very much behind the note written when I was that age. She emerged quite early in therapy, usually in a fairly typical sullen teenage manner. She seemed to hold a lot of the depression and anger the rest of us could not express. Jane would often come out (and still does) to voice anger and indignation at what she perceived as injustice. It took a very long time for her to trust our therapist enough to talk about the memories she held, or the grief she was carrying, but eventually her story unfolded. Jane had emerged at around the age of fifteen to step into the role she had been groomed for as a priestess within the group. This meant, amongst other things, being expected to take an active part in rituals involving sacrifice. At first it was seen by her as a way of protecting the corporate us—to be proactive in the group meant that we were less likely to be the ones getting hurt.

Things grew complicated when I began dating a boy in our neighbourhood. At first it was a chaste affair, mostly consisting of long dog walks and deep discussions about English literature (a passion for both of us). But then the fumbling first kisses grew into heavier and heavier petting, culminating in a desire to "go all the way". What I, the part around in the day, could not understand was the inner terror this brought—so much so that my boyfriend labelled me as frigid and eventually angrily dumped me for someone else.

This coincided with a crucial time for Jane. One of our main roles within the group had been as a "breeder" to produce foetuses that could be aborted and sacrificed. Around the time of the split with the boyfriend, we were in the early weeks of pregnancy. The group were unsure if I had actually slept with my boyfriend, and so decided to abort the baby earlier than usual, as it was considered potentially "unclean". For Jane this was devastating. There was no ritual honour in the abortion, and she was forced to stab the tiny foetus herself and swear to stay loyal to the group. From being a respected priestess with at least some recognition, she was treated with anger and disgust for her "betrayal" of the group. Deep depression seems to have set in at that point for Jane. This spilled into my daytime life, without any conscious awareness of why.

Two years later she had regained some of her status, and was again made pregnant by one of the leaders. This time she had been determined to obey the group, and gain honour. But when the time came for the abortion and the ceremony she panicked and tried to escape, bringing down more anger and scorn even as the baby was ripped from her. A few months after that I made the decision to become a Christian. This was the final straw for the group, and for my parents, and Jane was stripped of her role as priestess.

It is little wonder then that when Jane finally trusted the therapist we were seeing enough to speak, she presented as a very angry and depressed young person. She was also full of guilt and remorse for the things that she had done, and the role she had taken in the group. At first a great deal of time was taken allowing her to tell her story, and to weep and to rage at what happened. There was, and still remains within Jane, a huge sense of injustice at what was done. She had tried to be loyal to the group, to excel at all she was taught, and to gain approval. She was not believed by them, and she was not able to stop me from sabotaging all her best efforts by becoming a Christian. Jane was isolated, alone, and full of self-hate. But Jane was also full of grief for the babies she had killed, and most of all for her own babies. There came a point in her journey when it was suggested that a service be held to commemorate these babies. At the time it was me who needed to acknowledge them and to allow grief at their passing, but it was something Jane needed too.

In the church I attended there was an acceptance of the need for services for those who had miscarried, to acknowledge the loss of a life, and the grief that brought. This extended to those who had abortions. So it extended to us. The vicar sensitively arranged a service to mark the passing of the two babies, and to commit them to God's care. Whilst it was a comforting thing to do for me as a Christian, it was significant for Jane too—to have her babies acknowledged and her pain recognised.

Jane began her own spiritual journey of facing her past and her role, and questioning God in the midst of it all. She found it very hard, nearly impossible at first, to believe she could be forgiven let alone accepted by God. Perhaps strangely, it was never whether or not to believe in God's existence that was an issue. The turning point came when she recognised that what she was clinging to was the desire to be accepted and loved by Mum and Dad, and by the group. Once she realised this was never going to happen she was able to begin to let go and to dare to look instead at where there might be acceptance and love in the here and now that I live in.

Jane began to ask searching questions of anyone who would listen— my therapist, the vicar, and Christian friends. She did not pull punches, and had very clear ideas of right and wrong, of justice and injustice. But eventually Jane came to a point of recognising for herself the grace of a God who died for us, and decided, for herself, to give herself to him. This was no easy step, nor was it taken lightly. As Jane was quick to point out—she was not going to commit herself to anyone or anything again easily, and certainly not if there was any danger of re-abuse. To this day she remains my fiercest internal critic of anything said in church or in Christian circles that might hint of that.

Jane's need to make her own spiritual journey has been very real. Others internally are on that journey too, and are all at very different stages. Some are distinctly anti-Christian. But all need to be heard equally, regardless of my own beliefs, and given the opportunity to explore what they believe for themselves.

I have often been questioned by other Christians about the different "parts" that make me up. Describing to anyone how DID occurs and how it works as a survival mechanism, can be difficult. Trying to describe different person parts and their need for their own spiritual journey to some Christians can be even more difficult. Surely I was meant to be one whole person in Christ? Surely that is what I should be aiming for, rather than encouraging fragmentation by not only giving these parts names but also encouraging them to make their own spiritual journey? At one time this was what I believed too, though with hindsight I now wonder if it was more to do with wanting to fit in and get things right, and be the good girl.

But as my journey has unfolded I have come to view things differently. We are all, DID or not, made up of many different facets. The person we present as at work is very different to the one at home or the one being a parent etc. A necklace is a whole necklace but it may be made up of any number of different colours and types of beads. The difference between someone with DID and someone without is that the connections between the beads are not there. But all the beads are still needed to make the complete necklace that is the whole person. So we are each as human beings, one person, made up of many parts.

How can different parts exist who are not in agreement with the whole, and are not Christian? We all have parts of our lives, facets to ourselves that we prefer to keep hidden from others and, if we have a faith, then from God as we perceive him. But no matter how bad those parts are, they still make up the whole that is you or me.

In the Bible there is a passage that I have found particularly helpful in giving an illustration of this. It can be found in 1 Corinthians Chapter Twelve, verses 12–26. In this passage the apostle Paul describes how the body is a unit but is made up of many parts. Each part needs the other to be able to function as a whole. One part cannot say it does not need the other, or does not belong because it is not as good as another. Indeed the parts of our body that are "less presentable are treated with special modesty". Also, if one part suffers, the whole body is affected. Paul goes on to relate this to "the body of Christ". When we become Christians we become part of the body of believers that, in all its diversity and complexity, makes up the church. It doesn't take much knowledge of history to see how badly the body of the church suffers when its members war with or deny each other.

So I see it as vital that we accept the different facets, person parts, fragments, alters, whatever label you may wish to use as part of what goes to make up the whole person. More than that, we need to allow each part to make their own spiritual journey into understanding where they fit in the whole. I think that the spiritual journey is every bit as important as the physical and emotional one that has to be made in recovering from abuse and trauma.

Survivors who have been through satanic rituals will find making this spiritual journey very hard. Within satanism, Christian values and rituals have been inverted and twisted into very different meanings to those held by the church. So things like communion, candles, crosses, circles of people, robes etc may be extremely triggering, and very difficult to be a part of.

I have met differing views on this. Some survivors who have a faith choose to find different ways of "doing church". They may avoid things like communion, or devise different ways of worshipping that are meaningful and safe for them. To some extent I have not had that luxury as I am the wife of a vicar. For many years I would try to avoid certain services in our church, or slip out at the uncomfortable moments. But I made the decision eventually that I was not going to let the evil of the past dictate what I could and could not face forever. I found ways with each frightened or triggered person part of explaining the true Christian meaning of something like communion, rather than the twisted version they had been made to take part in.

Each internal part has needed to understand at a different level depending on their age, beliefs, and background. For some identities eventually that ritual has been redeemed and its true value restored. For others there is a need for them to know they do not have to be around or take part if they do not want to. It is very much a work in progress. But the important thing has been to wrestle with the issues rather than avoid them, and being prepared to acknowledge where each and every part is up to.

Working with DID presents many challenges. The challenge of working with the spiritual aspect of all that has been survived is just as important as every other aspect. Indeed I would suggest it is vital in any journey of healing from trauma and abuse.

CHAPTER FOUR

Reading, writing, and reeling

Oriel Winslow

S tudents are well-known for their chaotic lives: for burning the midnight oil, drinking too much, living off baked beans to pay for gig tickets, and for thinking that traffic cones make appropriate front-room furniture. And in many respects I was a normal student who faced normal challenges. I ran out of money before the end of term, ran the drama society, had chair races down the corridor, went to Budgens at 3 am in my pyjamas, and once started an examined essay four hours before it was due, and only noticed after I had handed it in that it contained the line "the flower imagery is very flowery".

But alongside this I had another, differently chaotic and frightening life, which the "normal" chaos of university life often camouflaged. I have dissociative identity disorder. As well as the I that I am aware of—the student who had achieved As at A level, was excited about starting a new course and meeting new people—there are many other personalities residing in my body, who therefore share my experiences, and who at the time I was unaware of. This made my life at university incredibly complex. In addition to all the usual difficulties faced by students, trying to mix student life and DID creates a myriad of other problems: What do you do about lectures if someone is around who is too young to read? Or when the subject matter is triggering? What do you do when you have to finish an essay by the morning but someone else is determined to kill you before the night is out? What do you do when one of your four-year-olds starts screaming in the middle of a seminar presentation and you have no idea why? What do you do if you have an alter who was told by her abuser that she was "asking for it" when she wore jeans and therefore freaks out when you don the student uniform of jeans and a hoodie? What do you do when someone decides to deal with the fear of being raped for failing an exam by not going to said exam? Or when one of the little ones has become so attached to a faculty member that she won't let you function when they are off work? How do you explain to your tutor why you, who have just presented a mature, insightful argument in her seminar, are now sucking your thumb and unable to function?

Chaotic as this may sound, at the time it wasn't even this clear. I didn't know about the others, and so when something happened such as another alter running out of a seminar, all I really knew was that I was no longer in the room, and other people were asking for explanations I didn't have. I got very good at covering up, saying things like I had suddenly needed a drink or had received an urgent phone call in an attempt to make my life look slightly less crazy. Sometimes I really believed what I said, sometimes I was too frightened to fill in the gaps and simply moved on to the next thing. Other times I was vaguely aware of things, such as being very upset if I had to change seminar groups from a tutor I was attached to, but didn't know the reasons for the strength of my reactions and so could not adequately explain them to myself or anyone else.

This may seem strange—how can I not have known that there were other personalities sharing my life and routinely taking over my body? I am often asked this question. By design DID allows a level of functioning away from conscious horror of the abuse, which allowed me the student to exist. And from my point of view I was only consciously aware of the parts of life that I was present for. DID on the inside looks very different from the outside—I was not aware of the switching because I literally was not there to witness it. I sometimes think of it as looking at a photo of the outside of a house, while standing inside it—the two are not immediately recognisable as belonging to each other. I was aware that something was not right, but had no idea what it might be.

Also, and I am more ashamed about this bit, I often did not want to know. Some bits of my life worked, and I had little inclination to examine the parts that didn't, thinking instead that if I tried harder at the bits that did, then the other stuff would just go away. I don't think much in life really works like this, and DID certainly doesn't. But having a fractured identity makes it very difficult to get a coherent sense of what kind of person you are, what you like or are good at. So when I realised I was good at studying, I held onto that as hard as I could, ignoring as much as possible all the bits that got in the way. Unfortunately that was only me and the others had little interest in academic achievement. They had their own needs and wants and identities and understandably wanted these met as well.

This essentially meant that our entire undergraduate years were spent as a battle for the body. By day I would be the student whom the department soon had their eye on as a potential PhD student; by night, when I was tired, the others were more triggered, and we were away from public observation, they took over. This resulted in nights of no sleep, refusing to get into bed, a desperate starving four-year-old trying to get fed by stealing other students' food, enacting oral abuse by inducing vomiting, binge drinking to numb the pain and self-harming every night.

Sometimes by day the more prominent alters came through and my body was taken over and driven by their needs and understanding of the world. We were anorexic, which exacerbated the need to steal food at night, as our four-year-old felt even more starved in the day. And when confronted by other students who understandably wanted to know where their food had gone, I genuinely said that I didn't know, and thereby earned a reputation as a liar which compounded old messages and did nothing to ease the confusion.

If the subject matter triggered us too much, an alter forced the body to miss lectures. And because I was dissociated, I didn't consciously know what was triggering. A lot of literature is about sex and power in one way or another, and the discussions in seminars often touched on things that upset people inside, and I did not have enough awareness to try to choose sensibly.

We became intensely attached to any member of staff who showed care or concern, often with disastrous results. The staff member thought they were offering a bit of support to a mature, slightly fragile twenty-year-old, and didn't understand that they were also offering it to a very traumatised child. This is one of the parts of our behaviour that I am most ashamed of. Lecturers are not there to give emotional support.

They do not anticipate having to give it very often. However, although my adult knew this, my alters did not. They sought out support and care wherever they could. Although this is hard to accept, it was also necessary for them to survive that period; our therapist at the time was not offering what we needed, and as I pushed my alters down, their needs did not disappear just because I wanted them to. Children's needs do not disappear because the adults are busy. My younger alters' attachment was very damaged during the abuse they experienced, and they were trying to get those needs met. Much as it may have annoyed or confused the faculty members, it was probably this care and support that allowed us to get through those years.

In theory I had a therapist at the time, but she certainly didn't pick up that we had DID. I think she felt her main role was to keep my functional part functioning. This may have helped me get through the demands of my degree but, if anything, increased the split between my student self and my more disturbed parts. The more chaotic my life got, the more I felt I was failing her and so I hid it as much as possible. As a result our therapeutic relationship broke down, and meant that later when we did go to another therapist my alters felt they would be pushed away again if they came out, and so did not even try to communicate with her for years.

Sometimes I did try to get help from other places, but I got very frightened every time anyone suggested a psychiatrist, believing at the time that it would rob me of what I had managed and could achieve. I believed that if I "gave in" to the more disturbed parts I would lose everything. I knew there was a lot in my life that was working. And even when I did accept help it was far from straightforward; even on the most superficial level it is very hard for anyone to help someone with DID without knowing what they are dealing with. For example I was given sleeping tablets, but did not know, at that stage, that we had been drugged during abuse and taking them made certain alters think we were being abused, so inevitably they made the nights worse. I was referred to an eating disorders unit, but the alters who were driving that behaviour had very complex reasons for feeling it was unsafe to eat, and did not want help, believing that they were keeping the body safe by keeping it underweight. They therefore invented food diaries, refused to let the body go to appointments or, if I did manage to get us there, didn't appear in sessions.

University is a very permissive environment in many ways. Bizarre behaviour is not uncommon. Chaotic behaviour can therefore go unchallenged or dismissed as eccentric. It is not unusual to see people passed out in the corridors. No one really thinks to stop and see if it is a drunk member of the rugby team, or a dissociated five-year-old spaced out on sleeping tablets that have triggered a flight reaction and now does not know the way back to her room. My department overlooked unusual behaviour, choosing rather to focus on my grades. And most of the time this allowed me to also ignore the more difficult aspects.

It can also be a very holding environment. My degree provided a structure that we desperately needed and although the subjects I was studying were often difficult and triggering, in retrospect I also think they held something important for us. Sometimes the courses I chose were driven by a need from inside. For example, I chose to study children's literature and wrote my assessment on Hans Christian Andersen's *Snow Queen* and J. M. Barrie's *Peter Pan*, discussing the needs of the children in both books to grow up in order to achieve safety, and the sinister dangers intruding on the world of seeming innocence. Similarly I wrote my final dissertation on presentations of a fragmented self in modern female poetry. The very thing that was painful in these subjects I think also unconsciously held something that was not being held in therapy. However, the line between something difficult being explored in the safety of literature, and something being too triggering for the system to tolerate is a very fine one, and I certainly didn't know my system well enough (or at all) to know where that line lay.

My university had excellent pastoral care services. These provided just enough day-to-day support to contain the disturbance that spilled out; the counselling service normally had emergency appointments and the health centre was open 24 hours a day. However, both of these services were designed to be surface level support, their brief being never to dig deeper; so while they were a life saver to me time and time again, they added to the emerging theme that disturbed parts could be patched up and ignored while I focused on the "real" aim of getting a degree. The split originally created by DID was reinforced by me, by those trying to support me, and by my desire to survive university. Without this I don't believe we would have survived those years, but trying to maintain functioning through that level of splitting very nearly cost me my sanity.

But we got through, just about. I have a first-class degree of which I am very proud, and a love of literature that will stay with me for life. I also have some very traumatised alters, and some behaviour towards them that I am far less proud of.

I started doing a Masters, and everyone, including me, expected me to go on to a doctorate. However, things started to unravel very fast. The experience of a postgraduate is much less holding and much less structured. I was no longer living on campus and therefore did not have regular access to the support that had been offered me. My friends had moved on and so were not there to help to keep me in the present. Our flashbacks became more intense and intruded on the day more, our eating disorder became worse and gradually it became impossible to get to lectures, let alone do any work in between, and it became obvious that an MA was no longer manageable.

Around this time I also changed therapists and began to work with one who understood that the roots to my problems lay in trauma. This was vital as it finally meant that we were talking about the right things, but it also brought terrifying feelings to the surface and meant that maintaining life in the present became very hard. Trauma took all of my time, attention, and energy. The level of splitting meant that the study was not possible.

This was an extremely difficult period. Therapy was uncovering a lot of painful things and unravelling the defences that had aided my survival and functioning up to that point. I lost one of the aspects of myself that I valued so highly—my ability to study—and I felt I was floundering in a mess of flashbacks, alters, memories, and feelings I had no idea were there. It definitely felt that it was all getting worse, but it also felt that it was what we needed to be doing. Because despite my pretence that everything was all right, I knew somewhere that underneath it really wasn't.

Socially all this was very challenging. My friends and acquaintances knew me as articulate, functioning, and capable. I had to fight for what I needed against a background of expectations that graduates with first-class honours degrees do not live on benefits and go to therapy three times a week. But we do. And I also didn't want to believe how much was wrong and how much we needed, which meant that whenever someone questioned me or challenged me about how I had suddenly gone from being a high achiever to being barely able to function, it fed into my own negative messages that I "should" be different, "should" be studying, "should" be able to put the past to one side and carry on. As my peers moved on into the adult world the background of student chaos was not there to camouflage and absorb my behaviour, and it became harder for both them and me to tolerate.

For me, things began to turn around once I finally realised I had DID and got a formal diagnosis. I know that some people find the notion of a diagnosis difficult and pigeonholing but for me it was vital to begin to make sense of my confusing and frightening behaviour and think about how to manage my system. Without this I do not believe I would have been able to go back and finish my MA, which I did three years later. In order to do this I had to completely reassess my relationship with studying. The MA could not be the focus of my life—it had to be done in the context of the fact that the others were profoundly abused during childhood and still lived with that as a daily reality. I therefore had to let go of the drive to get a distinction. I found this harder in many ways than dropping out altogether, as my ability to do well was such an important part of my identity. It is painful to accept that my skills and interests could not be fully realised because of the needs of the others. But I had to learn to see the bigger picture and put it in context; given the choice between learning about theories of linguistic narratives, and comforting a five-year-old who is having a flashback of being sadistically raped, the choice suddenly becomes simpler. One of the hardest things that I have had to face about our time at university was that through trying to stay a top grade student, I denied them their needs for food, help, and their own space.

Even knowing all this, and changing my perspective, did not make studying at this level straightforward. Sometimes going to a two-hour lecture meant hours and hours of preparation. Our little one needed extra food, as she still associated studying with being starved. The others needed to be resourced and reassured that going back would not mean a return to old battles. Additionally, living with DID is unpredictable, something can get triggered that needs all of the therapy time, induces hours of flashbacks, and means we simply can't meet deadlines. I still struggle to learn this, and to not get annoyed if I have set aside time for something and it is needed for something else. But this is the legacy of my childhood. If the others were not there to hold the abuse, I would not even have A levels. Set next to that, turning up to anything is a massive achievement.

All of this was very hard to explain to my tutor. She saw me highly functional in class, but did not understand that it may be the only two hours I got in the week. She understandably felt I was not fulfilling my potential, and she was not very interested in understanding why. The disparity between how I often looked and the reality of what I was living was one of the hardest things to explain. I once told her I wouldn't be in the following week as I was in a crisis centre at the time, and she said I didn't "look" suicidal. Faced with this sort of reaction it was so hard to remember what we all needed and not fall back into self-judgement, that I was just being difficult.

But on the whole I did manage to a much greater extent to take on board that our past had to come first and that every day we needed to live as *we*, not I. The smoothest periods in fact were the times I was able to include them in some way in what we were doing. For example, one of my violent alters, who was most unsure about being able to tolerate the MA because she was very triggered by the idea we were "pretending" everything was all right, found the process much easier once we agreed together that my dissertation would be on violence and language, and that she could be involved in tearing up books and researching violence. Because then I was not only engaging with an MA dissertation but also with something that was central to her life.

It was certainly not all plain sailing and there were very rough patches. On one occasion a peer was presenting her dissertation to the class, which turned out to be on pornographic films and feminism. This included showing a part of one of these films, and one my alters fled in terror without any shoes on, and ran out of the building into traffic. To make matters more complicated, there was an entry code on the door to get back in which she didn't know.

I do now have an MA but it is not as good as anyone expected. The fact we have it at all is a huge nod towards how well we now work together most of the time. And for us the fact that we do not have a distinction is, privately, actually a much bigger achievement, although that is still hard for me to remember sometimes.

I have decided not to do a PhD for the moment, because despite our collective success, my internal family still need the vast majority of my attention every day. I am very proud of what we managed and it was healing and important to go back and complete what we had started, but I am less happy about some of the ways I did this. For example, I sometimes bribed some of my little ones to stay out of the way while I studied, along the lines of "if you let me do two hours work then we can go to the newsagents and choose a toy". This is a huge improvement on refusing to accept that she was there at all, and was an important part of our process, but it makes me uneasy when I think of it now. I do not think any outside child should be bribed to stay quiet, although obviously treats have their place. However, life is not perfect, and I could not put everything off until I had finished therapy and learnt to communicate with my alters "perfectly". Sometimes whatever gets you through is good enough. But I do not think this is OK parenting in the long term, which is one of the reasons I did not stay on to do a PhD. It felt a bit too close to ignoring them again, if a little softer round the edges. We also could not fully attend to healing and an MA at the same time, and certain alters were put on hold. They deserve the chance to heal, and for the moment I need to give them that above all else.

The other issue, which I have only recently identified, is that it was only me who had the interest and the level of education required to undertake a PhD. The others are younger, interested in different things, and need their own time. Taking on something as huge as a PhD is a massive thing for anyone, no matter how stable and how committed. And I do not have the luxury of having my brain the whole time—I share it with many others, and so it is not really surprising that only having access to a percentage of the time in the body conflicts rather with the level of commitment that a PhD requires. It would of course be possible, actually essential, that I involved them where I could, in terms of choice of subject as well as arrangements about study time, but it still would mean that the body's biggest commitment, apart from maybe therapy, would be to something "I" had chosen. In terms of internal group dynamics, at this stage of our process that seems to me to be a recipe for disaster. As each of my alters has engaged with therapy and come out of the past enough to realise there is a present, they too need time to develop and engage in their own interests. Many of them already resented me for a whole host of reasons (no pun intended!) and to take on something so huge, which would mean a massive commitment from all of them to support me, would be too much for our system, in terms of how our relationships with each other are developing right now. It may of course be very different in the future, but at this moment in time it feels against the grain of what we are collectively trying to do. There has to be space for the others if they want it, and not just in therapy. One of the alters started attending a pottery class. Another chose to spend time making jam. And although I may not directly relate to these activities, they are just as important, and in many ways just as big an achievement, as studying literature was for me.

I have recently begun talking to my therapist about how the split that exists in my system between host and alters, which was so vital for a time in my life, is not very conducive to moving towards co-consciousness or integrative functioning, as it requires artificially pushing them away when we have to function in the outside world. This is exhausting and can result in a pressure-cooker environment from which they erupt, and is not very representative of how we live. It also denies them the things that they can do and skills they can develop. Not that they should be obviously out if it is not appropriate, but that is different to committing to a postgraduate study that would ask them to go away for large periods of time.

A few months ago we started another course, a diploma in horticultural studies. A far cry from literature perhaps, but more in line with my system as a whole. One of my little ones loves gardening, and although she is not old enough to attend the classes, she feels respected by the fact it is an area that she is interested in and can, in her own way, relate to. This means she is more supportive of the system attending, and does not need particular resourcing in order to do so. It is also academically at a level that means that several of my older alters can actively participate. It is more in tune with where we are as a system at the moment.

But this undertaking has certainly not been without its challenges, and has thrown up things I hadn't even considered before. Certainly the act of trying to share it out has been complex. First of all I had to try to explain a bit to my tutor, especially as some of my alters sometimes attend as well as me. I have never before been in a situation where I had to explain to someone who needed to know, as it directly affected her, but was not trying to help me with it therapeutically, and had very little experience of the field of trauma. I still don't think she really gets it, but she is maybe beginning to accept that we are "different". We have also had to grow a different sort of thick skin, and accept that she will not fully understand and actually it is not her place to understand; all she needs to do is to accept to the best of her ability.

Also, on a daily level it throws up other problems, each relatively minor on its own, maybe, but adding up to some fairly big questions that I certainly don't have the answers to. For example, I had to do an exam the other day, on a subject that one of my alters had attended the teaching for, but was not around on that day. In an ideal world, the alter who attended the teaching would be the one to do the test, but we are still a long way from living in an ideal world (if there is such a thing in life with DID). Equally, a lot of the units are cumulative knowledge, and so to attend one day without having been there the previous one requires a lot of fast reading, thinking, and covering up. Obviously we need to learn to pass knowledge to each other somehow, but if we knew how to do that we'd be a lot further on in therapy, and life cannot be put on hold until these things are achieved. I also worry about other things, like will the external assessors notice that our handwriting changes from worksheet to worksheet? And if so will they challenge it? And what on earth would I say? Is it even OK in the eyes of the examining board for different alters to be doing the work? At the end of each practical observation we have to sign a sheet saying what we have achieved. Who signs that? And by which name? It is a bit strange to be changing names throughout a course; on the other hand the reason we have chosen this course is because it supports the more fluid functioning we are trying to live with, and interests many people inside. The reason I have left academia for the moment is because it was too difficult to not allow my alters to be out and engaging, but does that mean that they need to use their own names, or is asking them to sign in my name contrary to what we have been trying to achieve recently?

Some of these may seem like simple questions, many are not, but all of them have much bigger implications in terms of our relationships with each other and the outside world. It has highlighted things I never even considered when I was the only person in the system engaged with studying.

I have been trying for a while to find a way of writing a conclusion to this. And I have started and deleted it several times. I think this is because there are no simple answers. There is no one way of studying well (or at all) with DID; or if there is, I haven't found it yet. All the way through our various relationships with studying, the way in which we have had to engage with it has had to change in line with where we are in our process and our specific needs at the time. I am sure that will continue.

CHAPTER FIVE

The role of friends in recovery

Carolyn Bramhall and Deborah Briggs

"If you think you're too small to be effective, you've never been in bed with a mosquito." Friends often feel "small" when it comes to effective support for those who have been severely traumatised. However, we have found that non-professionals can play a hugely important role.

Therapists are restricted by availability and professional boundaries. Friends are usually available and by keeping and maintaining healthy boundaries could be extremely valuable. When it comes to those with dissociative disorders, friends are often warned off from too much involvement for fear of doing further harm. What a shame!

Our planet is full of people. Due to their horrific experiences, survivors can be forgiven for believing that only bad people exist. However, there actually are good people out there who want to help, to love, to demonstrate that the world can be a beautiful place.

We each hold our own truth. Understandably, survivors may be extremely wary of disclosing truth of abuse to "ordinary" people who may not know what to do with what they hear. This is a reality but also is the human need for connection.

Often those who genuinely love them are the last to hear about their big, horrible secret. The fear is, if they know me will they still love me?

Can I cope with the level of being known? I wish I could say that all people will be non-judgemental, will be supportive and not see a person with DID as mad. But there is hope.

This chapter is all about hope, how friends can help with the survivor's recovery journey from a nightmare faced alone, to a voyage of discovery shared with safe people.

Healing has no fixed path. Just as no two people with DID have suffered the same or have the same psychological makeup, each person will have different goals and these need to be respected by all.

We have seen some people with DID reach their goal of integration with no professional intervention at all, as well as those who have had the close support of a therapist. Each person can decide what help they will seek and accept. Sadly this may include only what they can afford. Professional therapy is not cheap and has no guarantee of being helpful. The significance of supportive friends is of value beyond price.

Carolyn reflects

In the sticky issues of separation anxiety and attachment that can be so raw, therapists can put help and supports in place. Christopher, my therapist in the early days of my own healing journey, made audio tapes of his voice—reading stories to the child alters and talking me down when I was panicking. But they only kept things ticking over. An awful, black feeling would descend upon me as we neared the end of the therapy session. I would dread the moment of parting. I would do anything—*anything*—to prolong the session. I cannot begin to describe the agony of loss when the door closed and I had to walk into the scary, harsh, unfriendly world outside, with no prospect of being with another "safe" human being for what felt like a lonely and painful eternity.

But suppose, on closing Christopher's door, a trusted friend had been there to welcome me? Someone who had some idea of what had been going on in the session, and would happily hear about it, if and when I was ready to tell. Someone who understood exactly what I needed to do next, and so we would head for the coffee shop for chocolate cake, or to my room for a long sleep, or to the gym for an energetic workout. A part of the world, however small, would have existed for me that was safe, kind, and strong.

Deborah reflects

Are you safe? Are you not afraid of pain? Can you put your hand on your heart and say you will stick by a person with DID regardless of their sometimes bizarre behaviour? Do any of us know the point at which we fail to be all we hoped to be for another? What is important is the intent and also self-care. I believe you need to be safe to offer safety.

The opinion of the counselling community tends to be, still, that DID clients require specialist knowledge. This is changing, particularly with the growth of the survivor movement and specialist "experts by experience" trainers. However, although there are now many more therapists taking on dissociative clients, there is real concern over ritual abuse, or those with more severe symptoms.

Limited professional resources is a reality, so one suggestion is to equip "ordinary" people to take on a substantial role in supporting and caring for this client group.

Back to Carolyn's story

Keeping hidden

A survivor will have very good reason, of course, for keeping knowledge of her dissociative disorder from friends, and often family too. One woman I know is determined to keep the truth of her past and her present struggles from her husband, as she feels it would overwhelm him and he would leave her. But it is backfiring, as her depression is deepening and he is unaware of what is happening to his wife. He accuses her of secrecy and doesn't understand her need to spend large amounts of time away from him and their two young children. Other partners may simply not want to know or cannot face knowing. Each DID survivor faces a different dilemma.

As for the critical period during recovery when memories are surfacing, and new alters are making their presence felt and known, to have friends around you who have some knowledge of what is happening, and can listen to your rantings without fear—that is priceless. I (Carolyn) know what it is like to be able to simply chat about the characters you have inside, and knowing that somebody can in some measure share in their ups and downs is hugely helpful.

How do we equip ordinary people to effectively help

Carolyn, as director of Heart for Truth has the immense privilege of equipping people who want to be just that, a good friend. Four main areas need to be addressed.

1. Working as a group

It is important that support and encouragement is not offered by a "lone ranger". That leads to an unhealthy, intense relationship and too many demands to handle. The survivor's needs become overwhelming, the complications of transference and attachment can swamp the friend, and her own needs can become entangled in the web of relationship strands with alters. The need is for the friend(s) to know themselves well enough to be able to have a good guess at what they may be able to manage and to be open and honest about that.

In my experience there has to be more than one friend: it is really important for the survivor to see herself as part of a group, belonging to a community of friends; that it isn't all about her. The group approach offers an opportunity not only to be loved and heard and supported, but also to be appreciated for what she has to offer to the others in the group.

I am finding that having friends who are "there" for the survivor really works. People who understand the dynamics of DID, and who know enough to put appropriate boundaries in place in a positive way, can be immensely powerful. It helps if friends learn together with the survivor, so she knows what they know and what they don't, and can inform, explain, and amend as necessary.

Let's be clear that we are talking about good, old-fashioned friendship, not do-gooders—buddies who will hang on in there, ready to have a laugh, but who will also not be overly alarmed when the laughter turns unexpectedly into tears; people who also want to include their survivor-friend in their lives. These relationships are a world away from the dark corridors of memories, and can provide a welcome relief and a healthy diversion. These friends can keep a sensible eye on practical things like diet, sleep, fresh air, recreation, and the like.

There are pitfalls to be overcome of course. As a friend I have to face the frustration of the survivor's apparently unmet needs in spite of all my best efforts. I must come to accept that I can't fix it for her.

It is confusing when nothing seems to work and I may sometimes be offended and hurt when they are angry and take it out on me.

However, I can play a part in creating an environment in which the survivor can begin to relax and to feel safe (whatever that might mean in reality for her, though that particular word may not be the right one to use). Then it is inside that caring, enclosed community of friends that she begins to find herself, take risks, and see the world in a different way.

Being a part of a friendship group or team dilutes the intensity of relationships, and completely alters the dynamics of the survivor's impact. I (Carolyn) have been setting up supportive teams around Britain and, latterly, Europe, for almost ten years now, and I never cease to be amazed at how self-sacrificial and incredibly kind many people are towards those who are struggling in their dividedness. Wherever I go, which is largely inside the Christian community, there are good people who want to help their friend who appears to be acting oddly or breaking down or not coping as she used to.

They may begin with a sense of hopelessness, often a reflection of the survivor's own feelings, and may even have all but given up, on the verge of cutting ties with their hurting friend altogether. However, once they are on board as part of an informed team they seem to swing into action and find a new energy and a new loyalty. Once they have come together to form a supportive friendship group, however small, a new enthusiasm is created or an old enthusiasm revived. There is an energy that ripples around the group—"we can do this together, we will see our friend whole and well".

2. Training

But how on earth can "ordinary" people even begin to be a serious force for good in the life of a survivor, even to the point of becoming a main player in the recovery journey? The key is for them to understand the dynamics of the dissociative process and, where appropriate, ritual abuse.

I cannot stress enough how important it is that we educate the general public and in particular those who have a key role in the life of the survivor. The victimisation of children appears to be increasing though it is almost impossible to measure. I predict we will soon arrive at a place where the number of survivors seeking help far outweighs the therapeutic resources available (if we haven't already reached that place). It is time we began to rigorously spread news and information about the effects of ritual abuse and dissociative disorders to the general population. We need to see people equipped to be "safe" friends who are not afraid of those whose inner turmoil and conflicts see them presenting with otherwise unexplainable behaviours. Taking action in this way could potentially change the face of the way we approach those in trauma recovery, but action is the key word. As Edmund Burke famously wrote: "All it takes for evil to triumph is for good men to do nothing."

When friends (and perhaps family) are helped to grasp the dynamics of dissociation—why it is there, how it was formed, the function it has had in the survivor's life—so many things fall into place for them. They are no longer in the dark. They may have felt that their friend had been keeping something from them, which of course they had, and felt rejected. What a relief to have a feasible explanation for the mood changes, the secrecy, emotional outbursts, sexual desire or lack of, not to mention the more extreme behaviours of self-harm, suicidal ideation, or even apparent psychoses and unreasonable fears. At last they feel "in the loop" and part of the story. A fundamental change occurs in the way the survivor is regarded.

Therefore the survivor will need to talk about what they think would help in any situation, and honestly say where something does or does not work—she needs the opportunity to really be listened to. At some point a gathering together to discuss these things, perhaps with someone who has trodden that path before, is advisable.

It can be useful for all members of the team to read a book, attend a seminar, or listen to a talk that will inform and educate. Then they can come together to talk about how they can be helpful in their particular situation.

An introduction and explanation of the dissociation process can be part of the teaching. The person in the street is more open to new and seemingly bizarre information with the coming of the information explosion. Therefore when teaching about dissociation, and in particular DID, I am sometimes met with scepticism; occasional incredulity, but seldom disbelief. It all makes such sense. It ticks boxes. It provides a feasible explanation for why their friend, loved one, colleague behaves the way they do.

I met Jane (pseudonym), who had DID, together with her husband and a group of friends from her church. The couple were in big trouble financially, their marriage was failing, the children were unmanageable, and their friends worn out. Everyone was utterly at a loss as to how to understand or help. Her alters were appearing at unplanned times, and she seemed to be obsessed with evil. The usual agencies were on the scene to help—CPN, GP, social workers—but the different strands of support did not appear to be joining up, and the resulting chaos appeared to be overwhelming for Jane.

The dissociation dynamic was explained and reasons offered for Jane's various behaviours and struggles. Then we looked at the role of each person present, and how they would contribute to Jane's sense of safety. When the whole subject of satanic ritual abuse, DID, and the recovery process had been outlined and chewed over, a sense of enormous relief settled on the group. Jane's husband's reaction was particularly significant: he was thrilled to have an explanation that accounted for why his wife behaved the way she did. Their relationship was completely renewed. Jane saw no therapist but with the support of her now knowledgeable and sensitive network of friends she was able to work through the issues that were underlying the fragmentation. Jane is able to return to work and she is now helping others who are in emotional pain in her church.

Friends are so grateful when they come to understand this amazing coping mechanism. It is so immensely logical. Of course a small child will want to escape such yucky and confusing situations. If you can't just disappear on the outside, then you will have to go away on the inside. Their view of the survivor changes; she is no longer the problem, she is the hero! They feel privileged to be part of her journey.

Explanations about ritual abuse have to be delivered in a non-sensational way, without any hype or emotion; just the facts. People react in different ways. Most, when hearing about it for the first time, understandably feel shock, revulsion, and perhaps temporary unbelief. But as it is presented in the context of a fact-based teaching session, backed up with anecdotes and stories, it is usually well received. There is horror and repulsion over the abuse, but not at the survivor-friend.

Sometimes involvement with a survivor stirs up things for a friend and old memories are triggered. Can one victim/survivor help another? I believe that a deep sense of unity and camaraderie is created as one survivor recognises another. Firm, clear, well thought through boundaries need to be in place, of course. There will need to be others in the group who are able to maintain balance and introduce a basic level of "normality" to their corporate relationship.

3. Knowing your role

How is this group of friends organised to effectively help a survivor in recovery?

The key is in communication and delegation—knowing who does what and when. Each member of the group only does what they can do; nobody tries to do something they are not equipped for. So anyone supporting a survivor will need to understand what it is that they can offer—and stay with that. In terms of thinking ahead and counting the cost, it is important to appreciate the difference of the survivor's world. Survivors often have very practical needs, such as lifts to appointments and shopping trips, company in the evenings, advice about diet or budgeting, or the opportunity to participate in voluntary work. People to talk to or laugh with, and who will go to the cinema with them, are real assets for the survivor-friend. Just having fun could be the role of one friend (a very necessary part of the therapeutic process) while another offers practical help in the form of lifts, or financial advice.

Sue (pseudonym), a young woman with DID, spends time every week with a trusted friend, Carrie (pseudonym). They talk together, with alters coming and going. Occasionally a memory needs to be worked through, or an issue addressed. Carrie is not a counsellor but she does understand the dynamics of the dissociative process; in fact she has seen another friend through the process and into complete integration. Carrie and Sue have been meeting together for a couple of years now. Other friends understand what kind of "stuff" Sue is facing, and are supportive of them both, as Carrie also needs time to off-load occasionally. Sue feels safe with Carrie; she can say what she needs to say.

Carrie is safe in knowing there are others who understand what she is doing. The child alters are also secure in Carrie's affection (and with some other friends). Sometimes Sue stays overnight, and Carrie's family have met some of the alters, seeing it as quite normal and acceptable. They also know that one day Sue won't need these inside people, when she is ready to integrate completely, which is what she really wants. They are surrounded by an informal group of people who understand, and Sue is making real progress. But it isn't just a one-way street. Sue also helps Carrie clean her large house, and is happy feeling that she is giving something back. This scenario would not be right for everyone, but it is right for them. Carrie and others like her do not change their lifestyle and routine to accommodate their survivor-friend; rather, the survivor is embraced and included in their life.

Can the deep-seated and complex issues faced by a survivor of satanic ritual abuse really be adequately addressed by non-professionals? Every case is different, and each situation has its own set of challenges and resources. My personal experience is that some, like Carrie, are able to call into being inner resources, and with sensitive care and clear boundaries they can and do recover. Others need the intensity of a professional therapeutic relationship. But all could benefit from having the solid foundation of reliable and understanding friends who support each other. Even when the issues are more complex and things are largely dealt with in therapy, for example where mind control has been an issue, friends still have a vital role to play.

What does caring look like in reality? Perhaps to have had to stand by and watch as DID friends get involved in unsafe activities with unsafe people, and be there to pick up the pieces afterwards. You could find yourself as a friend travelling at 3am to a maternity hospital to help a survivor through labour and supporting her as her first and second children were taken into care; or receiving calls/texts in the middle of the night about suicide attempts. In the event of a crisis such as a suicide attempt it may be good to explore this *before* it arises; then both parties know what to expect (to a degree) from each other, rather than receiving a shock or feeling betrayed if a friend calls 999.

Jo (pseudonym) has DID in addition to a number of physical disabilities. She has a group of good friends who ensure she has adequate lifts to the shops, hospital appointments, benefits office etc. She is much loved and admired as the inspiration she is in her bravery and courage in the face of horrific memories and accompanying messy personal circumstances. I am in awe of the sacrificial love that Jo's friends and many others are prepared to offer these survivors.

When it comes to alters, some people may feel out of their depth. However, things change with experience and understanding. I am constantly amazed at how well "ordinary" people cope with the appearance of an alter and come to relate to them with great wisdom and sensitivity. They are encouraged to speak in age appropriate ways to each alter, with no great fuss or fanfare, within a previously agreed time frame, and very quickly relationships can be formed. But not every friend has to meet alters, and survivors may not want to be vulnerable to certain friends in that way. The relationship each friend has with the survivor is totally unique. It is the *quality of the relationship* that can be healing. Primarily the value we offer to each other is in who we are rather than what we do.

4. Equality

There are some who approach the helping role with an attitude of superiority. They will have their own reasons for being in that place, and so it may be necessary to help them to change—it needs to be spoken up front that nobody in the group is in any way "better" than another. There is no place for a patronising attitude towards the survivor. She may have very obvious problems to work through, but *she is not a problem, she is a friend*. Nor is she to be put in the middle of some well-meaning but misinformed circle as the poor victim requiring kid-glove treatment. She may be particularly vulnerable at this moment but things will change. It is vitally important that everyone, including the survivor, agrees that we give and receive as each is able. She is a human being of great value, and whatever has happened in her past in no way negates what she is today, but rather equips her to build on the depths she has developed through her suffering.

I started a group at one church, and one of the first things the survivor did was take everyone out for lunch! The tone was set at the beginning, and even though in the months to come the team needed to offer a lot of practical and emotional support, she was able to give something back. That helped her to maintain her dignity and self-respect, and balanced out some of the less dignifying aspects of recovery.

What does it look like from a survivor's viewpoint? Being respected, honoured, believed, trusted, loved—these are things that gradually pervade through the whole system and help her to feel an increasing measure of security. As safe people in her life offer consistent care, as she is included in the lives of others as a valuable contributor and not just the "problem", as she is called upon to help others as well as being helped herself, there will be a sea-change. Something dawns, a kind of awakening, and the strength that is fed to the core personality, and in turn to individual alters, feeds the whole system. It takes strength to keep going in the process of memory work, stabilisation, alter management, and the like. Where will the strength come from? It could be from the company she keeps.

There is so much a friend can do that a therapist cannot. In terms of learning how to live life "out there" therapy just doesn't tick all the boxes. As valuable as it is for the survivor to talk and work through the memories, to give time to the alters to tell their stories, to provide that unique therapeutic relationship, there can be no real substitute for someone physically by her side, to talk her through difficult practical situations, to give immediate praise for each small victory won, actually there, on the spot, in the flesh.

The advantage that non-professional support people have over professionals is that they are still there when work colleagues have gone home for the day. In the difficult night hours there could conceivably, with forward planning and appropriate boundaries, be a friend on the end of the phone. In a crowded shopping centre, when triggered, a friend could be present when a professional would not be. When a hug and a hanky is all that is required, there would be no uncomfortable professional boundary issues or rules to negotiate.

Deborah reflects

I have needed to consider my role as a friend but also a therapist. None of my friends with DID have been my clients. I have a level of understanding but still a human tendency to be cautious. I like friendships to be two-way and my friendships with DID survivors are no different; just at times one side may need more support. I have found being vulnerable and being there while another is vulnerable can cement relationships. I have a great deal of love and respect for my DID friends.

The reality is that a therapist is protected to a degree by the professional boundaries; we care but the strength we have is in not being a friend. A wise person once explained, as a therapist I am available to the client for that session but to a friend I would be very unlikely to give so much attention! The roles are different; neither is superior. If I had to choose I would rather a person with DID had all the supports in life we all value—security, stability with family and friends, those we love and who love us. The goal of therapy is healing and an ending; the goal of friendship is healing and unending.

I do appreciate the strength that many DID survivors draw from being a member of a church or spiritual family but wisdom is important. Sadly I have also encountered gossip, betrayal, and manipulation.

It is simply wonderful to build these friendships but at the same time to have a sense of caution.

Yes there are situations that are difficult for untrained people, when nobody knows what to do next. Challenges can be stepping-stones or stumbling blocks. It's just a matter of how you view them.

Friends can model coping skills, give immediate feedback, hang on in there from one end of a dissociative episode to another. Survivors don't just have crises within convenient office hours. But friends can be there, and often are, when the counselling office has closed for the night, and the emergency hotlines only offer the faceless voice of a stranger. The truth is that the people left facing the crisis are the ones that professionals would say are not equipped to deal with such things. In reality, they have to deal with it, equipped or not.

I help form groups that include the fragmented survivor and stick with her throughout the recovery period. Their tenacity is based on a genuine love, and a good grasp of the dynamics at play—why she may self-harm or become unmanageable. This is taking place both with and without the presence of a counsellor or therapist. It is not an easy journey to take; some inevitably fall by the wayside but for those able to stick with it, the gains are enormous.

Can we really trust untrained people to effectively lead someone with DID into health? I believe not only that we can but that we have to, if real and lasting recovery is to take place within an acceptable timescale for every survivor. We have to if stable relationships within families and communities are to be maintained with the many wounded victims of our age. It means the survivor feeling comfortable within herself as a human being, and also in her relationships and her role in life, encompassing job, family, hobbies, beliefs, and spiritual and emotional work.

Recovery has to be set in the context of the whole of life. We cannot see somebody through to "full" integration or even, as some choose, to the management of alters, and think the story is over. It has only just begun. There is life after therapy. Fitting into the community (which knows little or nothing about what has taken place in the survivor's life) and entering the "world out there" becomes the challenge. Informed friends could help her navigate her way into the niche that is just right for her.

Someone wrote to me recently who, having integrated a number of alters alone, has now come to the realisation that she really does need help after all: "It has been harder than I had ever imagined ... I felt overwhelmed with grief ... I am working so hard at this and ... I have no one to ask." There was no one to bridge the gulf between what used to be and what can be. She needs some good friends.

Friends and carers who share the survivor's walk out of fragmentation, confusion, and fear into the breathtaking freedom of life as a single, whole individual, learn about working together, appreciating that where one is weak another can be strong. Each member of the team can have some of their own needs met simply by having a clear and important task within the boundaries of belonging. They learn that courage is contagious; pain does not have to last forever; they can smile even when it rains. They discover what enormous strength is released when a previously locked-up mind is allowed to fly.

People are hard-wired with a need for community. Part of the survivors' pain is often the crushing sense of isolation, the secrecy, the slammed doors where there should be welcome. There's an element of risk taking for both survivor and friend; the silence is isolating but it's a real risk. Transparency and honesty and the joining together of lives even in the face of adversity—especially in the face of adversity—creates a quality of life for all involved that is totally beyond what they could previously have thought possible.

There really are people out there who choose to share the lives of those who bravely walk the war-torn path from the dark, forbidden territory of abuse disclosure into the light of acceptance and a bright future. Friends play a vital role in recovery. Let's find them, keep them, and honour them.

CHAPTER SIX

Satanic Ritual Abuse (the painful truth)

Paula Bennett

W hen people think of satanic rituals it may conjure up images of Harry Potter, witches, wizards, Halloween parties, annual trick-or-treating, and other harmless, if strange, fantasy and fun. However, in the actual world of Satanic Ritual Abuse (SRA), there is no such thing as a treat, only evil tricks played on you by the very people who should be keeping you safe and secure.

I was born into a coven to a family spanning nine generations of witchcraft involvement on the maternal side and eight generations on the paternal side of the family. Most covens are family generated and high incidences of incest mean that members often cannot be sure who belongs to which family. Each month, a coven cult meeting of thirteen, twenty-four, or thirty-six members takes place with the leader—a high priest or priestess—and their master, Satan, to initiate new members or carry out rituals based on different phases of the moon.

On the coven calendar there are big meetings for events such as Easter, Christmas, and (the biggest of all) Halloween. These meetings are highly secretive and filled with sexual orgies, the sacrificing of animals and children, chanting and screaming in wild excitement, drinking, and drug taking. These are not celebrations, they are terror-filled, especially for the children who live in fear of rape, extreme physical trauma, and even the fear of having to watch or participate in the death of a friend. For three nights around Easter, children are shut in a closed coffin, and there is a Black Mass involving the murder of a baby, which is then burnt and eaten. Children are constantly kept in extreme anxiety until the next meeting, wondering if they will make it out alive.

But it isn't just the meetings that hold the threat of death or horrific harms of a physical, mental, emotional, and sexual nature. Every day you are alive you wonder if it will be your last. Everything done to you in a coven is a cruel, deliberate trick. Adults lead you to believe that you are the evil one, the one who carried out a particular ceremony, even though *they* force you into carrying out atrocities that are unspeakable and soul-destroying. They let you believe that you are the guilty one and any attempt to speak out leads to further punishment. The tragic part is that you are always being punished and never quite know what is right or wrong, good or bad. Every child in a coven is made to feel wrong, and is terrorised so much that they are too frightened to ask questions because that leads to further beatings or rape, often both. The worst thing for many SRA survivors is not simply what was done to them, but what they are made to do to other members of their coven. The sad and horrific truth is that not only are you a victim, but you are also made to be a perpetrator—a reality that for many, including myself, is the hardest part to come to terms with. We must hold on to the fact that what we did was done under duress, that we were puppets and the adults held the strings, that it was not our fault. No child can stand up to these people.

Your whole world, as a child in a coven, is based on lies, deceit, and absolute fear. The real truth sounds so bizarre that you think no one in their right mind would ever believe you even if you did tell them, and this is the horrific hold every coven in the world has over anyone who manages to survive SRA. For even the survivor ends up believing that the atrocities seen, heard, and experienced, must not have happened. Survivors may be so scared to talk that they split into another person just to prevent the whole sordid truth from being remembered. In order to survive, other personalities may be created to deal with the appalling trauma, which is what happened to me. I believe that far from being a disorder, though, Dissociative Identity Disorder (DID) is in fact a gift given to SRA victims or survivors to enable them to get through the evil atrocities and practices of the coven/family/cult into which they have been born. The actual disorder and sickness lies in the coven and the rituals and atrocious ceremonies its members are subjected to.

I believe that DID is a key to keeping one's self alive and as sane as possible. Dissociation is the main tool used to separate yourself from what is happening to you, and from what you are made to see, hear, or do. As someone with DID, you often have no idea who is running your inner system at any given time. The core person is the one who was there in their mother's womb from the beginning. If the abuse started at the very early stages of life the core person may not often be around. Other parts develop in response to trauma. These parts may be made to take on individual tasks or situations to spare the core person and main body from having to experience the trauma or torment.

Whilst some personalities may protect you to the bitter end, there are other parts who may act as loyal cult members. Often people with DID will have many different parts within them made for particular jobs within coven activity. Parts who are loyal cult members may feel it is their place to make sure the core person and other system members go back to the coven for significant dates on the coven calendar, whether they want to or not. Moreover, that particular personality may have other loyal followers inside them, or may terrify the younger children inside, telling them that they are going to a party especially for them, or that someone they love or care for will be killed if they don't go along. This is so cruel and, as I have experienced on many occasions, it usually comes to light too late to do anything about it, or any evidence is destroyed so that there is no proof of it. There is such deep, hidden deceit in a cult like this, and it keeps you so soaked in fear, that whether you are aware or totally dissociated from the rest of your body, you may not find out what has been done to you (or, sadly, what you may have done to others at the hands of one of your personalities) for weeks, months, or even years later. These personalities may feel so fearful that they continue to keep secrets.

My journey to diagnosis and help began in the year 2000 when things inside me started to resurface and I became aware that I needed more emotional help. Over the years I'd had many different types of counselling and therapy, but I was not feeling any better and becoming increasingly unstable. I felt that I had to do something quickly before I lost the plot. I had recently joined a new church and each time I went I was feeling more anxious and frightened. One Sunday that autumn I went to the back of the church and asked for prayer as I was struggling with the communion service. It was here that the next part of my journey began as I was led to a lady who could pray for me, and I agreed to begin seeing a counsellor weekly to help with my deep issues of anxiety.

The counsellor and I began a journey that took both of us into the realms of the most horrific trauma and memories that left us both reeling from nearly every session. I began to tell her the threads of things that I remembered, stating that I had not been back to my family since I was fifteen years old when I was thrown out on the streets, living rough for two years. I explained my mental and emotional breakdown two years earlier, how I didn't feel like I was getting better and my belief that the mental health team did not know what to do with me. I was losing time and never really knew what I had been doing, where I had been, or why my body hurt so much.

I began to speak of my family and the pain my mother, Connie, put me through in the day and the physical, mental, emotional, and sexual abuse that she subjected me to at night. I explained how my father left home when I was nine years old and my stepfather, John, abused me from the age of ten. I also told her that I had a twin brother whom my mother adored.

Connie would lock me naked in the garden shed, chain me to a post, and make me eat and drink from dog bowls. From a very early age, she would make me bark if I needed anything. Day or night, warm or cold, I was forced to live with deprivation and cruelty that no child should have to endure. I was forced to sleep on a long table in the attic in just my knickers and vest, whilst my siblings were downstairs playing and laughing.

As I began to trust my counsellor more I felt safer to talk about the daily sexual abuse I suffered at the hands of my brother and stepfather. My brother would invite his friends over and they would pay him fifty pence or one pound to have sex with me, which Connie knew about and encouraged. Sometimes she would even join in, especially with her husband. On the day that Connie and John were married, John said that he now had two brides and that I was his special little wife.

Sadly, this was only the tip of a very black and frightening iceberg and I didn't know if it would drown me or make me swim harder. Even as a child, I knew I was different to those around me. As a child I was not allowed to choose friends for myself and rarely went to school. My birth father was in the army and so until he left home when I was nine years old, we travelled around the country and the world. In my little head, even then, there were always noises and people talking. I did not know what it meant and never questioned it as I assumed everyone experienced it.

I could never understand what made Connie hate me; she never showed the same behaviour towards my siblings and so I tried extra hard to be a good girl. I sought to protect my siblings and would take the blame if they did something naughty so that they wouldn't get hurt like I did. I couldn't comprehend why something that seemed right to me would still turn out to be wrong and would lead to me being beaten within an inch of my life. In the early days of therapy with my counsellor I often asked if I was in trouble, whether she liked me, and if she believed me.

A year or so into therapy, we both experienced a shocking introduction to DID when Poppy appeared on the scene. Poppy is three years old and was trying to crawl under the coffee table in the consulting room. Until that point, I believed that—following a long period of time with two Christian friends who prayed with me—Poppy and my other personalities had been integrated and that I was one person again. DID was not something my counsellor had experienced before but she managed to coax out Poppy from under the table, calm her down, letting her know she was safe and not about to be buried alive again in a coffin in the woods by Mummy or the baddies, as she feared.

We both began to unravel the pieces that had got tangled up into a web of deceit and lies told to me in order to hide the evil world I was made to live in. My counsellor enlisted the help of a colleague who attended one of our sessions and both were rather abruptly introduced to Sandy, my long-term friend inside. Sandy declared that she was not a "bloody demon" but the oldest member of my inner system at fourteen-and-a-half years of age and no one would get rid of her again. I don't think either counsellor knew what had hit them at that point! Sandy is a very angry and protective part of me. Although I did not understand for years the role that Sandy played in my life, I knew somewhere deep inside that she was the only person I could trust and who would never leave me. Sandy met me in my system when I was four months old and I recall seeing her one day when lying in my cot.

After this meeting and subsequent research by my counsellor and her colleague, as well as a long wait for funding, I was able to attend an assessment at a clinic in North London. It was here that I finally received the best present of all: a diagnosis of DID. After so many years of thinking I was some kind of freak, I found out that I was actually unwell and—most surprisingly—having had so many experiences of people not believing what I said, I was now totally believed.

I continued to see my counsellor and as a result of this diagnosis, I also began seeing one of the specialist therapists at the CDS who I continue to work with today. I must say that, had I known then what I know now—as a result of the hard work I have done over the years—I would probably have run in the opposite direction. I have lived and relived my past so many times that I feel older than my years. Some of the things I have discovered about myself still make me look back in horror. A major shock was to find out that Sandy was not the eldest of my personalities, but that some were actually older than myself. Indeed, when I say SRA is a life of lies, deception, and secrecy, I was not kidding. I have had to come to terms with many things that I took to be true but which have turned out to be much different.

I have had to come to terms with the fact that I am not the child of the mother and father named on my birth certificate, and that I am not a twin but a triplet. My real parents happen to be my maternal grand-mother and her father, my great-grandfather. I was not born in London, as I'd thought, but in the middle of Europe; and my date of birth was not what I had always believed. These are bitter pills to swallow. The woman named as my mother on my birth certificate is my half-sister and the "father" not related to me at all. It makes you wonder where, or with whom, you belong, if indeed you belong at all. I discovered that I have another sibling I have never met, and that the twin brother who abused me so sadistically has another sister. This other sister was given away to an "aunt", whilst my brother and I were given to Connie and her husband. Connie strangely loved her "son" whilst subjecting me to such atrocious pain and punishment, that I wonder how I ever lived through it, especially the daytime torment.

To this day, due to the things I experienced, I cannot set foot in a gar-den shed. I wake up with such horrific night terrors that I hardly sleep through the night and often end up needing to sleep with the light on. My body still hurts when I remember the things Connie did to me, and that's without taking into account what happened at night. Most of the time I did not go through the abuses at night, because other members of my inner system took those punishments for me.

Through the years of psychotherapy, further revelations have transpired. At the age of fifteen, six days after the birth of my baby son, on a cold and snowy Boxing Day morning, I was thrown out onto the streets. I thought I was finally free of the cruelty of my family. This was to be another deception I would have to face. My newborn son was taken away before I could hold him and in order to deal with the fear of whether he was dead or alive, I had to put him out of my mind. I was now faced with enduring life on the streets.

Little did I realise at the time, but this was not my first child. From the tender age of ten I had already had one daughter, two sets of twins, and another son. One set of twins and one boy were born as the result of being raped by my stepfather, John. It was normal in coven life to have particular females allocated as breeders. Given that my periods started at the age of ten, I was chosen for this awful role and forced into having babies every year who were then either given away to others to bring up or killed for sacrifice. One set of twins given away to another coven family is still alive today and one of the boys was brought up as my sibling; no one knew any different. Connie or other coven members often took me away during pregnancy so that it could be hidden. How I wish the Children Act had existed back then, but sadly it came far too late to help me.

It was only three years ago that this nightmare ended. Despite being in therapy I wasn't to find out until a year later that I had been raped and forced into an abortion. One of my older group of personalities was forced to keep an appointment to go to a special clinic chosen by my family for the abortion. It was only when a similar experience almost happened again that I found out. I felt utterly broken and betrayed as I thought that the personality who did this was on my side. I couldn't understand why she didn't confide in our therapists or understanding doctor. It was a devastating revelation. Indeed the saddest and hardest part of coven life is that members believe they have absolute rights over you. So many do not have the strength to keep away or the willpower to say "enough is enough!" I have had to lose so much over the years of being in therapy and have had to learn some very painful and hard lessons to keep me safe and—most importantly—alive. By choosing to stay away from the coven and by not giving in to the pressures put on me through various personalities, I have lost every so-called family member. I have not done it alone—through sheer determination and hard work I have trusted my therapists and clinical team, along with friends and other supporters.

Since last year my family decided to turn their back on me and ceased contact. However, I stand strong in the knowledge that I walked away first; they simply knew they had lost the war with me, and the battle to get me back. It has been painful but also extremely liberating to know that I am now able to walk around without looking over my shoulder, no longer too terrified to travel alone, or to pick up the phone without hearing one of their terrifying voices.

I am still on my journey and I am not so naïve as to forget that I still need to exercise caution, but the best bit of all is that I am now able to find out—with the help of my therapist—who the real Paula Bennett is, and this is what I have been waiting for my whole life. I know that I have changed and that I am getting stronger. I know, now, that there is a special place for me, that I can decide who my friends will be and they will be the family that I make for myself.

I would like to thank all who have walked this journey with me and still continue to do so. I would especially like to thank my dear friend Louisa for helping me with the editing and tidying up of this chapter, for her love and commitment to me, and most of all for believing in me and being a wonderful friend.

The biggest thanks I have is to my God, Heavenly Father and, more than that, the best lifeline I could ever hope for. To Him goes all the glory; without him I would not be here today.

CHAPTER SEVEN

Personal and societal denial

Carolyn Spring

I don't know who I am. I cannot be who I think I am, ungrateful recipient of a standard middle-class upbringing. I have dissociative identity disorder. I am a survivor of ritual abuse. I am Carolyn, Switch, Charlie, Leaf, Diddy, Yellow, Brat, and Shine. I am 100 others, maverick cameos in my stop-start life of conscious unconsciousness. I am me. Am I me? How do I know that I am me? How do I know that anything bad ever happened? How do I know that these memories of rape, of torture, of murder are not just phantoms on my eyelids?

How do I know that these feelings of rage and terror and horror and grief are not just chemical imbalances circling through my blood? Deep in my guts is the afterglow of trauma. Deep in my guts is a terror-stricken child. All day, all night—pain, the screech of remembering. I am infested with memories. They are like maggots crawling on the underbelly of my consciousness. They shouldn't be here, they're not mine—I am not the me that remembers. I am the ungrateful recipient of a standard middle-class upbringing. I am in denial.

My story about denial starts with myself at the age of four, a little girl with blonde hair and blue eyes, who was already being abused in at least three separate contexts. This little girl who was me was taken into some stables on a relative's farm and raped. Except ... she wasn't. This little girl who was me floated somewhere up above the straw and the horse muck and said, "This isn't happening"—or rather, "This isn't happening to *me*."

That experience of detaching from yourself is a common one for trauma survivors. It's often called dissociation. It's a thousand of those experiences that led to me developing dissociative identity disorder, this most surreal of labels that seems to mean, to me at least, "Nothing bad ever happened to *me*."

This chapter is about denial. There's the denial that I and every DID survivor seem to struggle with on a daily basis—"Did anything bad really ever happen to me? Am I making it all up?" And then there's the fact that we live in a society that wraps denial around itself like cotton wool—every bit as much as we do.

We live in a culture that denies that we're fat, or ugly, or old—we airbrush it away, have a facelift, dye our hair; anything but face reality. We live in a culture that pretends to be rich but really it's rich only in plastic debt. Our wealth is measured not by how much money we have but by our credit rating and our mortgage multiples.

We live in a culture of fake: fake boobs, fake tan, fake identities on the internet. We have hundreds of "friends" on Facebook but no one to go for a walk with; in cyberspace no one can hear you scream. We live in a culture of proxy—living our lives through soap operas, celebrities, and Hollywood romance. We play tennis on the Wii in our living room, not outside with a racquet and ball. We live in a culture of unreal, of fake, of pretend, of denial.

In 1994, 800,000 Rwandans were killed in 100 days of civil war. *800,000.*

Did you know that? What is that like? Can you even imagine it? What is it like for 8,000 people a day to be killed in ethnic violence—8,000 people a day, every day for 100 days? And the world didn't intervene. Back then it was in denial about what was happening and maybe it still is. There's no Ground Zero monument for these victims. We live in this Western world of "fun" and "excitement" and "glamour" and "stuff". Genocides can be happening in another part of the world and we don't even notice. In 1994 I was at university, worrying about essays, worrying about friends. Other people my age in a different part of the world were heaping rotting corpses into makeshift communal graves.

I didn't know that atrocities like that were going on. When I read the statistics now—800,000 people murdered in 100 days—I can't believe it. It doesn't fit into a worldview of iPhones and X Factor and the 2012 Olympic Games.

So it doesn't surprise me that we also live in a culture of denial when it comes to dissociation. It doesn't surprise me that people have never heard of DID. It doesn't even surprise me that the websites of many leading mental health charities carry no mention of dissociation and DID. Because we're living in a culture of denial.

It was that culture of denial that allowed my abuse to take place to start with. Did you know that it wasn't until 1984 that the Department of Health added the category of "sexual abuse" to its list of harms that can befall children? When I was being raped and made pregnant at the age of 11, it wasn't just my own dissociative process that told me that it wasn't happening; it was society too. "We don't have a category for that. Computer says no."

Judith Lewis Herman said "the ordinary response to atrocities is to banish them from consciousness" (2001, p. 1). So denial is the normative response to trauma. And denial and dissociation are two sides of the same coin. Remember?—"This isn't happening" and "This isn't happening *to me*." Elisabeth Kübler-Ross (2009) identified denial as the first stage of grief. That's why when people receive news of the death of a loved one, they think, "It can't be. This kind of thing doesn't happen to *us*." Cancer and fatal accidents are things that happen to other people, not to us.

And society has an embarrassing history of denial. In the 1960s family doctors appeared on adverts recommending particular brands of cigarettes. There was fierce denial of the growing proof that smoking was a major contributor to lung cancer and heart disease. The Holocaust was a humanitarian tragedy in which between five and six million Jews were murdered, and yet even today there are scholars who deny that it ever took place. The same was true of the AIDS epidemic in the 1980s, with denial from many quarters that HIV led to AIDS. It was scaremongering, they said, a moral panic designed to stigmatise and blame the homosexual community. And most recently there is denial of climate change, the "inconvenient truth" that our consumerist lifestyles are having a potentially catastrophic effect on the environment.

We don't want to accept these truths. They are uncomfortable, shocking and *inconvenient*—because they require us to do something. They require us as a society to change, and we don't want to.

And the same is true for child sexual abuse. Maybe one in four girls and one in six boys before the age of sixteen will be sexually abused, says research (Sanderson, 2006). A further twenty-seven per cent of women will be sexually assaulted in adulthood (Sanderson, 2006). What kind of society allows that kind of thing to go on and does so little to prevent it? What kind of society spends only the equivalent of a small chocolate bar on each sexual abuse survivor's recovery (Lantern Project, 2011)? You could be excused for thinking that it's a society that doesn't really care and doesn't really want to know.

So it *is* easier to deny it. Just as it was easier, I suppose, for the coroners and morticians and other professionals involved with Harold Shipman to deny the fact that so many of his elderly patients died during or shortly after a home visit from him. Doctors don't do bad things. Harold Shipman is a doctor. Therefore we will not accept the truth that a responsible, respected member of society, a general practitioner, someone in whom we place our trust, could have been Britain's biggest ever serial killer. How can someone murder over 200 people and no one notice? Because to steal Bowlby's phrase, "thinking what we are not supposed to think, and feeling what we are not supposed to feel" (1988, p. 99) is an uncomfortable thing, and is quietly but staunchly discouraged in our culture of denial.

The same, I suppose, was true in the Baby P case. Peter Connelly, blond-haired and blue-eyed, hauntingly beautiful, tragically killed. He died in London in 2007 after suffering more than fifty injuries including eight fractured ribs and a broken back. Yet he had received more than sixty visits from social workers, doctors, and police over an eight-month period. The serious case review into his death lamely concluded that hospital doctors were at times too willing to believe the parents' explanations for their son's injuries.

It's denial again: "This isn't happening." A father, a mother, do not hurt their child deliberately. That goes against everything that we believe a father and a mother to be. And it is that denial that is at the heart of the kinds of abuse that lead to DID.

It's the kind of denial that we as survivors have to engage in: Mummy wouldn't hurt me; Daddy wouldn't hurt me. Mummy loves me, and so does Daddy. I have a good Mummy; I have a good Daddy.

They wouldn't hand me over to other people to hurt me too. They wouldn't allow this to go on day after day, night after night, throughout my childhood. The reality of *that* is simply too much to cope with. We must deny it in order to survive.

And we feel such shame and stigma at the kinds of things that happened to us, that we don't ever want anyone to know. And we're told not to tell. In fact, we're threatened, we're terrorised, we're coerced and brutalised into never telling. So shame and secrecy become the perpetrator's weapons. It affords *them* the cover of darkness to continue with their abuse, and it leaves *us* alone and traumatised with no ability to fight back.

And when the kinds of perpetrators that I'm referring to are magistrates and doctors, teachers and lawyers, police officers and judges, when it's people that we rely on for our society to be just and fair and safe, is it any wonder that society and the media side with the strong ones against us, the weak ones, the mentally ill? Because, due to our traumatisation, we are after all a little "odd". We populate mental health wards, or we hide at home. We don't want anyone to know about our OCD and agoraphobia, our generalised anxiety and insomnia, our chronic unexplained pain and borderline personality. We certainly don't want to stand up and shout about it.

We've got through all these years by insisting to ourselves that we are the bad ones, the wrong ones, the shameful ones. And the rejection we experience too often, when we do tell someone, only seems to reinforce that.

If we stand up and speak about our symptoms and our histories, who is going to listen to us? Who is going to help? No one helped us back then; adults stood around and watched us be hurt. Who is going to believe us with our multiple personalities and our bizarre, scandalous allegations that it was the pillars of the community who raped us or tortured us? Would you believe the woman in the mental health unit over the smartly uniformed police officer?

And if we do speak out, we risk rejection and ridicule. I had a best friend once, the kind that you go shopping with and watch films with, the kind you go on holiday with and rescue when her car breaks down on the A1. Shortly after my diagnosis, I told her I had DID. I haven't seen her since. The stench and rankness of a socially unacceptable mental health disorder seems to have driven her away. That's the reaction we get sometimes. With others, they listen but they don't ask questions and they don't mention it again. I'm acceptable only as long as I don't act mad or mention abuse. None of my friends whom society would label as "normal"—the Joe Bloggs average person who doesn't need to be known as a "patient" or a "client" or a "service user"—very few of these would come to hear me speak at a conference or a workshop. It's just not acceptable conversation.

So am I surprised when a sixteen-month long police investigation against my abusers ends with "no further action"? Not at all. Do we really think that allegations against police officers and teachers and doctors and lawyers will result in a prosecution? Can I really be telling the truth when I talk of atrocities amongst the middle classes? If we can't contemplate the reality of 100 days of genocide in Africa, we certainly must deny the reality of ritualised, organised, extreme abuse in Middle England.

If society did not deny this, it would have to do something about it. Silence and secrecy are the weapons of perpetrators, but by default they are the stance of a society that doesn't want to have to face the "inconvenient" truth of dissociative identity disorder affecting up to 1.5% of the population (ISSTD, 2011). That's nearly a million people in the UK alone. We have a budget deficit. It's just not convenient to mention us. Not when the treatment of choice is individual long-term psychotherapy and not a drugs solution. If we could be medicated into a cure, the pharmaceutical companies would be fighting our case for us. But we require time, and a lot of it, from highly skilled and highly human therapist *people*. So really, denial of our condition, denial of our experiences, is the only sensible response that our society can make in a global recession, surely?

One problem is that we ourselves struggle with denial. "Denial of the syndrome is part of the syndrome," I often say. We all doubt our own reality. We doubt ourselves, our narratives, our lack of narratives, our memories, our lack of memories, our symptoms, our alters, our pain. Of course we do. Denial and dissociation are two sides of the same coin. We survived by denying. "This isn't happening"—"This isn't happening to me."

And our abusers rubbed their hands with glee. Denial is their defence too. We were taken out at night, raped, hung up, tortured, shamed—all manner of things that are too criminal, too abhorrent for words. And the next morning, sitting at the kitchen table, eating breakfast cereal in our uniform ready for school—did anyone mention it? Did we talk about it?

Did we discuss our reactions, our feelings, our fears? Did anyone help us to put narrative form around those events? Of course not. We ate cereal and drank denial for breakfast. We grew up fat, fed on a diet of denial. So is it any wonder that we developed denial-based patterns of thinking, that our brains grew up hard-wired into believing that *nothing happened*?

Denial is our very real, personal response to *our* own trauma. But denial is *the* normative response to trauma—by everyone. Society may deny that anything bad ever happened to us. It may deny that DID exists. But that doesn't mean to say it's right. All it says is that like global warming, our histories and our stories are an "inconvenient truth". The lack of treatment options for us is not our fault. It's just society reverting to a default position and denying that anything is wrong—while one baby Peter a week dies at the hands of caregivers, while a Harold Shipman kills the next patient, while someone else dies of lung cancer, and while global warming continues to wreak devastating floods in Bangladesh.

So what to do, then? Give up and accept that society will always be in denial about us? If I thought that, I wouldn't be writing this. But partly I am because there is a story from history that inspires me and encourages me. It is the tale of the abolition of the slave trade, and the stand that William Wilberforce took against societal denial.

Late eighteenth-century Britain *depended on* the slave trade. It wasn't just inconvenient to think of abolishing it; it seemed to many to be industrial suicide. The slave trade accounted for eighty per cent of Great Britain's foreign income.

When we look back from a twenty-first century viewpoint we can all agree that the slave trade was wrong. But perhaps we equate it to Eastern European migrants being paid peanuts to pick leeks in East Anglia. And that is a poor comparison. The slave trade involved immense human suffering. People were forcibly kidnapped from Africa and transported to the West Indies to work in the sugar plantations that made Britain 'Great'. Did you know that the British Empire was built on the backs of slaves? And those slaves were transported in the most appalling conditions, kept in "booths" hardly any bigger than a coffin, shackled to prevent them from throwing themselves overboard in despair. There was no sanitation—the spaces in which they were confined simply filled up with excrement and urine. Their joints were dislocated, twisted in unimaginable pain for three torturous weeks. Of the eleven million slaves who were transported by ship, nearly one-and-a-half million of them died—men, women, *and* children.

This was a human rights atrocity of the highest order. And yet in England no one batted an eyelid. At all. Our good friend Denial took care of that. Denial said that these black Africans were not even human. It's a different sort of mental gymnastics, but it's the same mechanism that allows an adult to rape a child. The reasoning is: this is not a human being like me, with feelings and the ability to feel pain, and emotions and desires and the right to choose; this is an object that I can use for what I want. And that's how the British people as a society thought of slaves—they are not human; they exist to meet *my* needs, *my* wants and *my* selfish desires. All that suffering so we could have sugar in our tea.

The second great denial was of the conditions on board the slave ships. They simply were not public knowledge. It was a "trade secret".

So what did Wilberforce and his colleagues do? They actually had a simple strategy—to raise awareness. And this is where perhaps we can see parallels today. How did they do it? They supported the publication of "survivor stories", the eighteenth-century equivalent of today's "mis lit". Freed slaves such as Olaudah Equiano wrote books and pamphlets, spoke out at public meetings and debating societies, approached prominent society figures, and pestered the press. His book was the bestseller of 1789, shifting an incredible 50,000 copies.

Thomas Clarkson, a prominent abolitionist, travelled the country gathering statistics, facts, and firsthand accounts. The campaigners lobbied parliament, organised boycotts, gathered hundreds of petitions, and even had a logo designed by Mr Pottery himself, Josiah Wedgwood. It all sounds quite familiar, doesn't it? But this was the world's first ever grassroots human rights campaign, in which people from different social classes and backgrounds joined together to put an end to injustices suffered by others.

It took twenty-six years of awareness raising and lobbying before the slave trade was finally abolished. It cost Wilberforce his health but he died, I'm sure, a happy man.

I believe we can do something similar. In the same way that the women's movement of the seventies and eighties brought rape and incest into public consciousness, we can do the same with the causes and reality of dissociation and multiplicity. But to tackle society's denial, we must tackle our own. There *is* a slave trade still in this country—yes, the real and horrific sex and human trafficking trade run by organised criminal gangs, which is appalling and *must* be stopped. But there's the hidden slavery too of children exploited and used within their own families, within organised and ritual abuse. And there's the hidden slavery of the tens and hundreds of thousands of us—maybe even the millions of us—who are slaves to secrecy and silence because we've been told that if we ever tell, then bad, bad things will happen.

And they're right. Bad, bad things will happen. To them. We were told not to tell because it protected them, not us.

How much telling we do must ultimately be based on what is right and safe and helpful for us all as individuals. I'm not advocating reckless, indiscriminate disclosures, or anything that will tip us out of our own window of tolerance. I'm talking about our corporate telling, our corporate assault on society's denial—just as the slave trade activists did when they dumped shackles and fetters onto the middle of the table during high society dinners.

That's what we're doing with this book. I'm speaking up not just for myself but also for all those who cannot yet speak up for themselves. If Wilberforce could demolish denial in a society heavily self-invested in the slave trade without YouTube or Twitter or Facebook, without email or podcasts or the web, just think what we can do with all this communications technology that we now have at our disposal. This book is about speaking out and letting people know that we will be slaves no longer.

Let me finish with a quote about Helen Bamber, the human rights activist. This is from an interview with Emma Thompson (Leitch, 2009) who said:

> Helen Bamber once told me that victims of torture have their voice taken away from them twice over. During incarceration and torture, they are deprived of a voice. Then, if they survive, often nobody wants to hear about what has happened to them. It's too disturbing. Thus, they lose their voices for a second time in the very place they may have expected to be heard.
>
> Some of them, having survived torture, cannot survive this rejection. What she has always said is that the hardest stories to listen to are often the most rewarding stories to hear. If you are interested in helping anyone, the simple act of listening is your first proper contribution.

The question is: are you willing to listen?

References

Bowlby, J. (1988). *A Secure Base: Clinical Applications of Attachment Theory.* London: Routledge.

Herman, J. (2001). *Trauma and Recovery: From Domestic Abuse to Political Terror.* London: Pandora.

International Society for the Study of Trauma and Dissociation. (2011). Guidelines for treating dissociative identity disorder in adults, third revision. *Journal of Trauma and Dissociation, 12*: 115–187.

Kübler-Ross, E. (2009). *On Death and Dying* (40th anniversary edition). Abingdon: Routledge.

Leitch, L. (2009). Interview with Emma Thompson. *The Times Online,* 5 May. [Retrieved 1 March 2011 from http://entertainment.timesonline.co.uk/tol/arts_and_entertainment/film/article6221077.ece]

Radford, L., Corral, S., Bradley, C., Fisher, H., Bassett, C., Howat, N., & Collishaw, S. (2011). *Child Abuse and Neglect in the UK Today.* London: NSPCC.

Sanderson, C. (2006). *Counselling Adult Survivors of Child Sexual Abuse (3rd edn).* London: Jessica Kingsley.

The Lantern Project. (2011). Prevalence Rates for Victims of Sexual Offending. The Lantern Project. [Retrieved 1 March 2011 from www.lanternproject.org.uk/articles/prevalenceratesforvictimsofsexual offending/50]

CHAPTER EIGHT

Living with DID

Carol Broad

*T*his chapter is accredited to Carol Broad, an individual who has
dissociative identity disorder, but Caitlyn, one of her many alters,
is undertaking this task on behalf of the multitude of identities that
together make up who we are.

Life as a multiple is never boring; we are all unique in our own
special way, as is everyone with a dissociative disorder.

If you were to look at me, you'd see a single person, a female in her
early forties; but when we look in the mirror we see *us*, fragmented
identities living within one body. At the time of writing we are twenty-
six alters each with our own distinct personality. When we delivered
our Living with DID presentation in March 2011, there were just seventeen of us, though we had grown from the original six Carol knew of
when she was initially diagnosed in 2008. Such is the reality of life with
DID. We are still growing as we discover further "hidden" identities
within ourselves. There are many terms used to describe an identity,
from parts to personalities, but we prefer the term "alters". We currently range from a small baby who is best described as "innocent"; to
Lucy, a precocious but loveable five-year-old; to Caz, a moody teen; and
to adult female and male alters. Sara is our most organised, and Toni

he's sports mad, whilst me (Caitlyn), well, I guess I'm determined and the others think I'm quite feisty, not that I'd disagree.

Our childhood

Life as a child was far from idyllic; we suffered severe prolonged trauma throughout our developing years. The only way we could cope with this was to dissociate from what was happening to us, believing instead that it was happening to someone else, not the light brown, blue-eyed child we were. This frequent dissociating in turn led to us developing the many and varied alters who now make up the person everyone else recognises as Carol Broad; many alters carrying individual aspects of the trauma we suffered in those years. But that ability to dissociate carried us through those years, enabling us to cope to some extent with what was being done to us.

We moved home and school regularly, to the point we lost count of the houses we'd lived in, the neighbourhoods and the friendships we formed that lasted just short periods of time. This chaotic family life resulted in many fractured relationships, which caused us many difficulties, not only as a child but in later life too. Our education was significantly disrupted, not only because we changed schools frequently, but as a result of long periods of absence, when our primary caregiver chose that it was best that we didn't attend.

We were a frightened child, anxious and desperate, and we were in turmoil by the time we became a teenager. We were suffering from mental health problems that required medication before we reached puberty. Benzodiazepine is a fairly regular feature of our life—medical notes show that we started taking them aged around ten or eleven. Medical professionals described us as a "poor, unfortunate child", noting there was very little they could do to help us. If only they had known the reality of our existence back then, maybe we'd be different today.

We felt great shame, guilty that we were not good enough to be loved by most people for the child we were. We held a great deal of hurt and felt very isolated; we were a neglected individual existing in a constant state of emotional turmoil. By the time we turned sixteen, we were desperate to leave home.

A verse from the Bible sums up those days: "We were hard pressed on every side, but not crushed; perplexed, but not in despair; persecuted, but not abandoned; struck down, but not destroyed" (2 Corinthians: 4).

However, we have to note it was not all doom and gloom, not all in those years was bad. We were fortunate that our father, "Dad", was an amazing person. He offered unconditional love that never wavered, to us his illegitimately born only child. Dad did not live with us all our childhood, he and our other biological parent were only married for a brief period. He and his mum, our Grandma, were both very kind to us; unintentionally oblivious to the reality of our existence, they enabled us to feel some of what we guess is a "normal" childhood. We enjoyed ice-cream sundaes with Dad, sang silly songs together, and played tennis and walked on the beach, on the regular, often too short visits. Grandma made us Angel Delight and taught us to sew and bake. Simple pleasures many would take for granted, that we absolutely adored and craved. We always knew that their love did not come at a price, it wasn't something we had to earn, or buy, but was mercifully free and overflowing.

Adulthood

We finally managed to leave home at seventeen, having met Philip, the man who later became our husband. At eighteen we bought our first home, settling down into some semblance of normality. We married a year later, on a cold crisp spring day, in our local church; we wore a wedding dress Dad had helped us to choose. He was the only man in the bridal shop but he never complained or felt embarrassed. We knew he was happy for us; he liked and respected Philip a great deal and on our wedding day he was most definitely the proud Dad walking us, his daughter, down the aisle.

We were happily married, though it was hard to explain or comprehend what "love" was or what "happiness" meant; they were mainly alien concepts to us. But those days were free of trauma and chaos, and that gave us stability like we had never known. We soon settled down into family life, being blessed with our three amazing children. Helen is a strong willed child who never was a girly girl, but is definitely the big sister and loving daughter. David, who is science mad and sadly suffers from an autistic spectrum disorder, is "Lucy's" best friend—he adores her sheepish smile. And finally there is Matthew, the youngest but not the smallest of the family, who is sports mad just like both his grandfathers. All of them are caring and considerate individuals, who have brought and continue to bring great joy and pride. We enjoyed a happy family life. Philip was and still is a good friend to us; we knew he cared for us and he was tolerant of our failings for many years. Dad was a constant presence, a real help that we needed greatly; and advice given by Philip's mum often assisted us to parent appropriately. We didn't understand how to be a mum, so her and Dad's guidance was really crucial, not just for us, but for the children too.

We worked in paid employment and in voluntary roles. We strove to achieve, to succeed, to be the best we could at all we did, desperate to ensure we were liked and respected as a person. Our voluntary roles developed over time and we guess we were career building along the way. What were initially local roles became regional and then national. We seemed to put on a smart suit and walk out of the house a different person; we could pretend to be this capable person, who everyone assumed was organised and confident. A far cry from the inadequate parent and wife we felt and knew we were behind closed doors. We know that it confused those closest to us, as we seemed to be two very different people living within the one body. It wasn't just a case of having a work role and a home role: putting on this facade for work, for the outside community, drained us greatly and often meant we'd return home and just collapse into bed, utterly exhausted. All that effort came at a cost.

Throughout the initial sixteen years until we reached the age of thirty-four we struggled with this balancing act. We were intermittently plagued with mental health issues, requiring medical interventions of differing degrees at different times but always as an outpatient.

At the end of 1999, suddenly and very unexpectedly, Dad passed away. His death hit us so hard. Our anchor, the one constant, consistent person throughout our life, was gone. We felt adrift and alone, despite the love of our family. We tried to be strong for everyone, especially the children. But Dad had helped us to hide the fragmentation of who we were: he'd deal with Caz's moody teenage tantrums, protecting the children from her outbursts; and the insecurities of the younger alters who he'd constantly reassure. He helped us cover up lost time, repaired the damage we physically generated, and emotionally protected the children; he took care of the tasks we were so inadequate at performing. Now suddenly it was down to us to try to keep this fragmentation hidden from those around us. It was a task we couldn't perform; the cracks in our facade began to show even more.

By the start of the millennium, we began to recognise things that soon became a part of everyday life—fragments of memory, flashbacks that developed over time. We suffered frequent nightmares, our sleep was disturbed and we were fast becoming an emotional wreck, closer and closer to breaking point. Our mental health soon began to deteriorate and by 2002 we were struggling in our role as a civil servant, as work was interrupted by the strains of this life. We began to self-harm; scars that will last a lifetime became a regular feature. We suffered suicidal thoughts and despite medication and counselling we made little if any progress. We found it difficult to deal with or comprehend the reality of what we were remembering of our childhood; what had been buried deep within our memory by the dissociation was beginning to resurface. We had no control over these times, feeling as if we were stuck on a runaway roller coaster, thundering faster and faster towards oblivion.

Harsh realities of DID

Though we did not know we had DID at this time, its effect upon us was very real and we suffered a dramatic deterioration in our mental health. In 2004 we experienced our first hospital admission, a frightening, surreal experience. Hospital was at this time an alien environment and an acute psychiatric ward wasn't a place we'd ever imagined we'd encounter. Sadly it was the start of many such admissions.

We were losing vast chunks of time, often finding ourselves in strange places with no explanation of how we had got there. We were by now totally unable to undertake any kind of work role, paid or unpaid. We seemed to suffer constant negative memories as we recalled past trauma, leading to us feeling inadequate and of no use to anyone. If anything we felt a burden and nuisance to Philip and our children, though they often told us otherwise. We felt totally unable to feel any emotions, feeling very detached from the world around us. Life carried on but we seemed to be stood still in an all-consuming pit of despair. We had hit the self-destruct button and couldn't release ourselves from its grip. Our self-harming behaviours grew worse and were by now a daily occurrence. We recognised that we behaved and felt differently at different times; as various alters began to be more prominent in our life we suffered from identity confusion. We no longer knew who we really were.

Suicide attempts and going missing seemed to plague our life; we were in utter turmoil and looking for a way out. We did not want these memories, we just wanted to have been loved by two parents and not used by one of them; and we desperately wanted to have had a real loving Mum. Looking back we know we burdened many professionals, from the doctors and nurses who cleaned our wounds and dealt with our desperation, to the police officers tasked with either finding us, or transporting us back to one hospital or another. We also know we caused a great deal of hurt and pain to those we loved the most, our immediate family. Philip and the children suffered much as a result: we led them to believe we didn't care about them—how could we if we wanted to leave them and die? Yet we loved them more than anything in the world, we just couldn't bear the intolerable memories or the pain these evoked inside us. No amount of saying sorry now will ever change the damage we know we did, but we honestly never meant to hurt them.

As one hospitalisation led to another, we seemed locked into a vicious cycle that was synonymous with the revolving door of mental health services. We were given a variety of labels, misdiagnosed by a multitude of professionals. We were labelled, stigmatised, and very misunderstood: we can still recall the number of professionals who felt self-harming was just attention seeking. If only they had realised the excruciating pain we felt deep inside but which we couldn't express in any words, which was why we cut. We just wanted to turn that emotional pain into a physical one, so it could be more bearable.

Our marriage to Philip broke down under the strain, as we spent long periods in hospital leaving Philip and the children to cope alone. Even those who love you have their limits of what they can take, how many suicide attempts that they can cope with. We were eventually denied the right to live at home with the children, as our constant harming was detrimental to their wellbeing. We spiralled out of control as the memories and the emotions these evoked plagued every waking moment. A teddy bear became a continual part of us as the younger alters sought comfort and security.

After many informal hospitalisations, we were detained under the Mental Health Act and formally sectioned in 2007. This loss of liberty, and the loss of the freedom to make choices that we felt were in our best interests, was gut wrenching. We couldn't comprehend why no one would let us escape this miserable existence and kill ourselves, but of course in hindsight we needed others to protect us from our irrational thoughts and feelings.

Our worst nightmare

It was decided we had post-traumatic stress disorder (PTSD) and as the acute but unlocked psychiatric wards could no longer contain us, it was agreed we needed to be housed in a more secure environment whilst we began to undertake trauma therapy. As Christmas approached in 2007, we were moved to a medium secure forensic unit some 223 miles from home. This was a desperate time for all of the alters (though we didn't see us as alters back then, just as us) and the family too. This forced separation from family and friends was excruciatingly painful. That Christmas was a very bleak one; we found it strange, especially when we realised that we missed the children. We'd never fully acknowledged before that we actually did have real emotions. We did have feelings after all, even if they were buried deep within us and seemed like unfamiliar concepts.

The secure unit was unlike any environment we had encountered before. We felt like a third-class citizen, forced to walk in front of staff, initially having to eat with a spoon and drink semi-warm tea from plastic cups, and deprived of our own possessions. At the start we were on continual observations, not even allowed the dignity to fully close the toilet door, or shower unobserved. For someone who had suffered trauma it was a difficult situation to find oneself in. We had lost any respect as a human being and we certainly had no autonomy.

The majority, though not all, of the people held at the unit were there under Ministry of Justice Mental Health Act sections. We knew that most of our fellow patients were people who had committed serious offences including murder. Yet some people were just like us, themselves victims of trauma who had been detained under regular Mental Health Act legislation. They had, like us, been committed to a forensic unit despite having no forensic history. Whilst most of the people we met were pleasant individuals it was clear many were very ill. There were constant outbursts of violent or disruptive behaviour, which terrified the younger alters we were by now recognising as a part of who we were. We thought everyone had different alters, were fragmented just like us.

Acts of self-harm on the ward were a constant occurrence. We found ourselves continually amazed, even shocked at how others self-harmed, realising for the first time how our own self-harming behaviour must have stunned and disturbed Philip and the children. Within less than a month we had decided we needed to try hard to stop our self-harming; we wanted to leave this place before it consumed us and our identity. Our time at this unit and the subsequent locked rehabilitation unit destabilised us as a whole. That dark period meant we were re-traumatised by the system that was meant to stabilise and care for us.

Yet we also made a firm friendship during this time that still lasts today, someone who judged us for who we are, who saw beyond our teddy bear hugging and recognised a real person. We valued their support in those dark days, and still do value the bond of friendship we share. Despite differences in age we have lots in common and when our fragmentation could no longer be hidden, that amazing friend treated us no differently, unlike many who seemed to think we had grown three heads. She'd comfort the young child in us who was crying, when staff ignored us not knowing what to do. She also enjoyed shopping or talking with the other alters that by this time made up the six identities that we were. It's a friendship we all hope and know will continue throughout the years to come, made in the darkest and desperate of times but that today brings great joy into our life.

Consequences

In the period from 2004 until 2009, we encountered seven different hospital establishments, from financially crippling self-funding at The Priory, to NHS acute psychiatric wards, to the privately operated forensic and locked rehab units mentioned earlier. In a period of five and a half years we were hospitalised in total for approximately 200 weeks. We became institutionalised, losing skills and hope. Shame and guilt weighed us down, as did the memories of past trauma. Suffering anguish, fear, denial, and turmoil, it's easy to see why we, like so many victims, feel to blame for their past. Even when we confronted some of our perpetrators, we were rebuked and made to feel like it was our fault anyway. The impact of childhood trauma is vast: trauma survivors have symptoms instead of memories.

Diagnosis

As our fragmentation became more and more visible to those around us, it was suggested we might have a dissociative disorder, something we had never heard of. It took months before we were eventually diagnosed with dissociative identity disorder. We had to secure funding for the diagnostic assessments, which for many is an extreme challenge in itself. The funding for the SCID-D (Structured Clinical Interview for DSM-IV Dissociative Disorders) test was less stressful for us though, as it was thankfully done as part of our appealing against our compulsory detention. In the end our appeal never did reach a Mental Health Act tribunal, as our "section 3" lapsed and we were allowed to become an informal patient, regaining some of our shattered dignity in the process.

But once diagnosed we soon realised that we then faced a lack of specialist services, having to *fight* for the correct treatment, *fight* for the funding needed, and even *fight* to be recognised for the multiple we are.

We soon realised that within the NHS, services for DID are quite simply a postcode lottery. We faced many sceptical professionals, who were and still are in some cases prejudiced against the diagnosis. They fail to comprehend the complexities of multiplicity except in a few rare cases. There continue to be regular battles, and at times it often feels like we have to climb Everest on a regular basis.

The one bright light in our life back then, though, was that for Philip and our children, the diagnosis that at first seemed alien to us made sense to them. It explained much about our previous behaviour; none of them was shocked by the diagnosis or fazed at what it meant then or now. Their love and acceptance is a valuable asset we know we are richly blessed to have. Many others with dissociative disorders that we have met are more isolated, unsupported, and alone.

Life with DID

In the cold light of day, having dissociative identity disorder has meant we constantly have to explain to non-understanding professionals the complexities of this condition that we now recognise encompasses who we are. We still suffer from flashbacks of trauma, encounter the crippling fear generated by body memories, and sleep is never easy as we frequently suffer from insomnia.

There is of course the regular, constant changing of moods reflecting the different alters that make us who we are. We are extremely forgetful, often buying the same thing not just twice, but often time and time again, before it finally registers with us all that we don't need any more of whatever it is. We hate the habit of forgetting partway through a conversation the topic we are discussing, caused through switching from one alter to another. We lose things frequently and need to keep duplicates of almost everything from keys to important documents. We also have to ensure other people know where we keep important items, as we forget that too. There are many triggers that frighten or alarm different alters, causing us to switch alter or in the worst cases lead to us shutting our system down by evoking dissociative seizures that mean we lose hours if not whole days.

Others tell us that each individual alter has their own quirkiness, habits, and individuality. We do not always recognise this, but over time we are now at least recognising some of the signs. Each alter has their own posture—Titch, she sits on her tiptoes—and clothing style—Toni, well, he hates pink! But CJ and Lucy, it's their favourite colour. We all have different annotation and vocabulary: Caz has a very northern accent; and me, well, we speak in a more refined businesslike manner, except when we get stressed. We have different writing styles and different alters write with different hands: CJ, she's left hand dominant; and me and Carol are right handed. Some of us have different eyesight, which is confusing and annoying when we suddenly switch and find we cannot see as well. It's often these physical changes that we notice more than the more subtle ones.

We switch frequently from one alter to another, usually without any warning, though we do have some co-consciousness between some alters. There are those alters we know through therapy that exist yet they do not know us and vice versa; there is just no co-consciousness between us. This all leads to what is best described as "internal chaos" and there are constant battles for control between some of the more dominant alters. Try studying when child alters want to play, or grocery shop if there's a toy aisle to distract them. There is constant pressure in living life as a "we", a pluralised existence in a non-pluralised world.

Light on the horizon

In 2009 we eventually received appropriate therapy, care, and support—none of this was easy. It was achieved with the help of those nearest to us, especially Helen and Philip, and the brilliance of a few significant individuals who care passionately about people with dissociative disorders or mental health issues and recovery.

Our future is brighter now. We receive inpatient care in the community provided by a unique mental health recovery care provider, Gray Healthcare. We are understood and supported appropriately, and are finally rebuilding relationships and trust, especially with our children. We decided it was best to ask them to treat us as a friend, rather than a mum, as some alters don't even recognise their children. Thankfully, with God's grace, they have been so accepting of us all. Their love seems to keep growing each time a new alter appears, and they accept us for who we are. We know we are very fortunate. We are learning lost skills, and relearning activities of daily living from cooking to self-care, though some things are still an uphill struggle. We thankfully live in our own home within the community, no longer institutionalised by a regime that failed to understand our uniqueness and our complexities. This is such a huge relief.

Yet we also live each and every day, not as a single being but as a *multiple*. We are a collective group of distinct identities, different ages, and different genders—each with our own thoughts, feelings, and ways of perceiving the world.

But we are still aware of doctors who fail to understand us or dissociative disorders. We face the constant fear that the health or social services funding that ensures our freedom, independence, and autonomy will be withdrawn. We are fully aware that there are potential further battles to be fought, as nothing in this world of funding and service provision is ever guaranteed.

Most impacting of all, though, is acknowledging we face confronting the past that we all desperately blocked out for so long. We and our family face the reality of comprehending the reasons why we have DID; all the connotations and implications that go with recognising and accepting we suffered severe trauma as a child. We are coming to terms with realising the impact of our past trauma and in turn our DID on those around us, the loss of parent–child relationships with Carol's three amazingly considerate, compassionate, non-judgemental, and understanding (young adult) children. The children have had to accept they have a parent whose best friend is a teddy called Theodora, and she has toys just like they did as young children. They have a parent who switches from adult to young child to moody teenager, all in less than a day. A parent who at times requires more care than they do, especially when the younger alters are more prominent.

Our future

We know we still have a long journey ahead of us; therapy is still in its early stages despite lots of effort on the part of us and our therapist. We are still meeting alters who have so far chosen to remain hidden away. Most times they bring past trauma or fears to the fore, things we find hard to comprehend but which we now have to come to terms with.

We have faced many pitfalls and negatives on our journey so far, but dissociation and dissociating gave us a methodology to cope with the trauma as a child. We have no doubt that skill probably saved our life back then, making it bearable for us to cope with the trauma we encountered.

However, we have to acknowledge that living with DID presents huge challenges; it is complex and complicated. But our diagnosis was the key to us accessing services and funding, which has enabled us to return to life within the community and to have a positive future. We can see constructive, productive elements in our life, and our faith plays a strong part in this. Whenever we feel in the depths of despair we recall words from the New Testament: "Those who hope in the LORD will renew their strength. They will soar on wings like eagles; they will run and not grow weary, they will walk and not be faint."

Our future can be brighter. We know that with the right help, continued treatment, and support we can potentially aim for partial or full integration. Yet even if this is not possible, whatever happens we can move forwards. We can live with the multiplicity of being an *us* and not a *me*, a *we* and not an *I*. We know that, as we are already living that life.

The future for people with DID and other dissociative disorders

Based on our own experiences, we know that despite the many challenges DID brings, with the right understanding, help, and treatment, all DID survivors can have a better future. So surely having to fight constantly for recognition, for understanding, and for funding to access the right care and treatment is utterly wrong.

DID survivors are failed twice: once at the initial point of their abuse/trauma and again when the system fails to acknowledge their needs, even doubting their diagnosis if they have been fortunate enough to obtain one. This cannot be right in the twenty-first century.

There needs to be a nationwide awareness programme for all NHS staff, to educate them about dissociative disorders. Diagnoses need to be more obtainable within the NHS; people's lives should be placed ahead of funding restraints and bureaucratic red tape. We need minimum standards of care and treatment agreed and implemented within the NHS to end the current nightmare of the postcode lottery—not just guidelines that can be ignored but actual regulations.

Those with dissociative disorders face a big enough battle living as multiples and dealing with past trauma. Like everyone else, they deserve to be heard and recognised, not stigmatised.

We know from experience that with Support comes Hope and Inspiration for New beginnings with Endless possibilities. People with dissociative disorders, including us, can and deserve to appreciate the sunshine in their life again.

CHAPTER NINE

Back to normal? Surviving life with dissociation

Rob Spring

We had been married for four years when suddenly everything changed: my wife "went mad".

For four years we had led a relatively normal life. We had been working together for two years as full-time foster carers; we were busy and active members in our local church; and we socialised as much as was possible with five small children in tow. Carolyn had always been very industrious, high-achieving and competent, excelling at everything she did. She was very level-headed, very much in control of herself, and very unfamiliar with emotional outbursts. She was a bit of a visionary, churning out a thousand ideas an hour, but she also usually had the expertise and the drive to turn those ideas into reality. I loved her very much, and life together was good.

So when everything changed, it felt like she had gone insane.

It all happened, literally, overnight. In April 2005 she suddenly had a breakdown. She had a difficult night, waking frequently with nightmares. In the early hours of the morning, I found her sat on the edge of the bed, staring into space, unresponsive, almost catatonic. And then she became upset. She was talking about things that didn't make sense, in half-sentences, incomprehensible, and bizarre. She became highly agitated, distressed, inconsolable. And I didn't know what to do. The next morning she awoke with a pounding heart and an unfathomable sense of terror. She felt as if she were locked in a room with a tiger with no possibility of escape. The panic, the distress, the huge waves of feelings that suddenly swamped her—we were both as bewildered as each other. Perhaps it was too many sleepless nights. Perhaps it was a build-up of stress from doing some particularly intense adoption work with our foster children. Perhaps it would just get better in a day or two and we would get back to normal.

We have never got back to normal.

Before long she started to feel that she wasn't in control of her feelings at all. She didn't even feel in control of her consciousness. She would lose time, not know where she'd been or what she'd been doing, find herself somewhere but not know how she'd got there, "wake up" in the middle of a conversation. During the daytime, she mostly managed to hold it together. As if with a flick of a switch, her emotions would turn off when necessary and she would continue to care exceptionally well for our foster kids. She would write reports, give evidence to the police, attend meetings, go to court. She would attend training and help deliver training. She would feed a baby and soothe a toddler and read a book to all five of them propped up or crouched around attentively, and everything would look like it was back to normal.

But normal didn't exist on an evening or at night. By 7.00 pm, when all the kids were safely tucked up in bed and fast asleep, she would crash. The professional, caring, competent person that she was by day would disappear, and I would encounter dissociation. I didn't know that was what it was called and I don't know if that knowledge then would have helped. There are things you can read about in textbooks, and then there are things that you can experience firsthand. And nothing prepares you for firsthand.

At times Carolyn would seem to just space out and disappear into her head for a little while, like a child engrossed in the telly. Then sometimes she would rock, like a neglected orphan, or for minutes at a time she would fall into a trance-like state as if hypnotised. She would "come back" again and not know where she'd been. And there was that look—that pained, hurting expression on her face, a terror in her eyes and a stiffness in her muscles—that told me that she wasn't just caught up in a report she was writing. It's hard to look into your wife's eyes and see pain so deep that neither of you can bear to put it into words.

I didn't know that she had "parts" or "alters"—dissociated, split-off parts of her personality. All I observed was my wife—my *adult* wife, this competent woman who I knew intimately and who was my best friend—climbing under the table, in terror, distress, and unimaginable pain. Then she would writhe and whimper and cry, and in a child-like voice would say things that would haunt me for years to come: "I don't like the ropes." She would gesture with her wrists, where *obviously* there weren't any ropes now. "I don't want them to come." *Who's coming?* I would think, and I knew that there wasn't a logical answer to that question *now*. But I also knew, instinctively, that there once was. "Don't hurt me." *Don't hurt me?* How could my wife, my lover, my best friend, this capable, competent, clever, compassionate woman that I'd pledged to spend my life with, this woman with whom I used to lie in bed at night and belly-laugh together about some silly word-play or a line from a sitcom—how could this woman now be so fearful of me hurting her? "It's me, Rob," I would say, as gently as I could. But she didn't seem to recognise me, and my presence seemed to alarm and terrorise her all the more. That hurt us both.

Her *littleness* was both confusing and convincing. Here was a little child speaking to me from an adult's body. At other times she would feel cold, so cold, so ridiculously ridiculously cold, and neither blankets nor duvets nor jumpers nor hot water bottles would warm her up. She would feel pain as if being cut with knives. She would feel dizzy and sick. She would feel that there was "yuk" on her face. She would taste things and smell things and feel things on her skin. And then came visual flashbacks too: of horrific abuse and people and places and things that evoked in her feelings of such absolute terror and helplessness that I knew that *something* must have happened to her as a child to cause such an abrupt and distinctive change in the woman I knew. When she "came around" from these episodes, she was disoriented and couldn't remember what had happened, or it was hazy and indistinct. Sometimes I would find her sitting on the stairs, rocking and totally unresponsive. Sometimes I would find her having just self-harmed.

I didn't know what to do. Perhaps typically as a bloke, I wanted to fix it. In my mind, at first at least, this behaviour was "wrong" and so it just had to stop. Inside I felt panic, fear, and anger. I wanted my competent wife back. I didn't want life to be like this. I didn't want this uncertainty and doubt to dominate every minute of every day. I didn't understand what was going on, and I didn't like it. I wanted to feel in control. I wanted to feel that this would all stop. I wanted to get back to normal.

My anger spilled out, at first, at her. The compassion that stirred in me at seeing her so little, so terrified and forlorn, was crowded out at times by my fear. "Just pull yourself together!" I would half-seethe, half-shout, in desperate, awful exasperation. Looking back, I wonder now how I could have been so callous, but I was bursting from the chronic stress of all those days and nights, one after another, on and on for months then years, of "madness" and terror and not knowing if I was going to come home to a corpse. I didn't believe in myself, that I had the capacity to cope with this. It felt unreasonable. I hadn't signed up for this—night in, night out of bizarre and extreme behaviour, my wife talking like a child, apparently delusional, apparently "gone mad". And then day in, day out, the continuation of our busy, stretched, stressful lives as foster carers to five very small and very needy children. But instead of *all* the children being tucked up in bed by 7.00 pm, that's when the "other children" came out. It felt like I was looking after kids twenty-four hours a day. And unlike with the fostering, there was no other adult around to help me. And I didn't know what to do.

So I withdrew. Foolishly, I let a friend come in and take over, and she tried to be our "rescuer". I stepped back, relieved that I wasn't alone in it all, but stupidly, mindlessly abdicating my responsibility. It was nearly the death-knell of our relationship. All I was communicating to Carolyn was that I couldn't cope, that I didn't want to know, that I wasn't willing to be there for her, that I didn't want to be anywhere near her when she was being "mad". A gulf developed between us and we both fell into the chasm. The "demon dialogues" began: whose fault was it, who was hurting more, who should solve it, why we didn't like each other any more. It's a pattern that a lot of couples know, right before they divorce.

And we stepped right up to the edge. We talked about it, we threatened it, we even made a decision. But it's not that we didn't love each other. We just didn't know what else to do.

Things got better *and* things got worse. I stepped up to the mark. I eventually realised and decided that my marriage was *my* responsibility, and my wife was my responsibility too. I had to be there for her. So we started to heal our attachment breaches, and I'm very glad that we did. Help came a year after the initial breakdown in the form of therapy with a very good although inexperienced counsellor. And our relationship started to change as I forced myself to engage with my wife during her dissociative episodes. I made a conscious and determined effort to commit myself to the woman I loved, even though she seemed to have been hijacked by a dozen or so other "people". As therapy progressed over the first few months, the traumatic nature of her childhood started to leak out, bit by painful bit. And then the memories of abuse started to pour forth as a deluge.

But they weren't related by the adult Carolyn that I knew. They were relived and re-experienced by what we eventually called the "little ones"—the child parts of her that had split off or been created to endure the repeated, overwhelming abuse at the hands of those who should have loved her. These little ones existed as if frozen in time, believing that the abuse was still ongoing, that the ropes were still there, the knife still cutting. They appeared often in the middle of the night, reliving awful physical pain, the "memory" in the body of the abuse and torture she had suffered. At the time they'd had no one to comfort or reassure them; they'd had no one to tell about what had happened. And so the trauma remained locked away and unresolved, unformulated in her mind, split off from her daytime consciousness. The only crossover into the daytime, competent Carolyn was increasing physical illness—intense pain, at times crippling, with no apparent physical cause, and stifling, continual nausea.

The evenings and nights were simply awful to witness: to watch her pass out repeatedly from pain, with little ones terrified and filled with a tangible dread that "the nasty people" were going to come and hurt them. Past and present were a bewildering mix. Often she could not bear to be comforted, and relief lay only in self-harm, in cutting and overdoses. These dissociative parts of my wife barely knew me. "Are you going to hurt us?" they would ask me, and it broke my heart. "Are you cross?" They found it almost impossible to trust me, even to get their words out, or to breathe. My nightly encounters with these terrified child parts gave me just a glimpse of the sickening atrocities to which they had been subjected. It would take years for the full picture to emerge.

The narrative developed in layers and often corresponded to developmental stages. At first, there were the little ones, parts of my wife's personality that were stuck at a pre-school level of affective and cognitive ability. One or two had names—Diddy just announced herself as if it was the most natural thing in the world for her to be called that. Others chose names to help distinguish them from the others: Frightened was always, well, *frightened*. Leaf used to count the leaves to distract from the horror of being raped aged four. Good Girl was the description of the one who came always to placate, to be good, to smile for the camera, to charm and elicit love. White Bear was a part referenced by a white teddy bear she had for comfort, which she clutched whilst passing out. Ditch Girl was the one who lay freezing and hurt overnight in the ditch. Yellow was … well, we never did figure out why she was called Yellow.

Then emerged some parts who presented as slightly older, late primary school, eight years and upwards. Charlie was the fighter who loved Manchester United, fierce and loyal and proud and terror-less. Charlie would beat you up if you tried to nick his football stickers. I would sit on an evening with Charlie and let him tell me obscure facts and stats about his favourite team, while he smoothed a sticker into place in his football album. Here was my 30-something wife huddled over some football memorabilia, talking like an eight-year-old boy, gabbling away about football, reciting information so extensive that it can only ever have been acquired to block out less palatable facts. There were a range of boys in this age category: "boys don't get hurt". Of course, *we* know that sadly they do, but that was the magical thinking that they clung to, in order to feel safer. They despised the little ones, the girls, for not fighting back. There was a lot of work to do on helping them understand one another, to value each other's preferred survival strategy.

And then there was Switch. I met him one night in the darkness. I woke to see my wife standing near the bed holding a knife. Or rather, *Switch* was holding a knife. Developmentally on the cusp of adolescence, male but in a sensitive, unassuming way rather than the bullish machismo of Charlie, Switch was anguished and deeply reserved. He felt everything keenly. He felt the emotions that adult Carolyn did not. He felt the rejection, the hostility, the pain. And he had turned to self-harm to cope. Switch was funny, courageous, introverted, daring, and shy. And over time—quite incredibly given his early reticence and obsessive reliance on self-inflicted pain as the only means of soothing and connection—he became the catalyst of Carolyn's therapy, and the hub through which all the parts began to integrate. At first my relationship with him was tenuous, with suspicion on his side, and a tendency to isolate. I felt uncomfortable too. Here was my wife, expressed in the form of a twelve-year-old, more male than female, but asexual, easily upset, and highly empathic. Switch was all the emotions of my wife rolled into a tight, dense ball of anguish. It took time to win his trust. But once I did, it was mesmerising. Switch and I watched football together, we watched eight seasons of the mini-series "24" together, we watched a thousand space and astronomy documentaries together. Switch came alive.

And through Switch's ability to connect to me and her therapists, those tenuous, threadbare linkages with Carolyn's multiple selves began to solidify and strengthen. Remarkable work was done in therapy. Remarkable narratives and reconnections were made. Remarkable atrocities were disclosed. Remarkable suffering was described. Here was a panoply of self-states describing and reliving and experiencing and communicating all the dissociated and split-apart aspects of the narrative history that coils together to form Carolyn. Most of it was mediated in some way by Switch. Even the big ones, the older, adolescent parts whose self-loathing was spun around a core of childbirth narratives—even they found a way out through Switch. Switch's integrative role was and still is central to Carolyn's healing, and Switch himself was enabled from the inside out, through relationship with me and her therapists, to learn to *be*.

But encountering in such a manner the extreme and organised abuse of children did not leave me unchanged. I have watched as through therapy for nearly six years the amnesia has slowly dissolved away. An inchoate narrative has formed, and threads have been drawn together from different parts of my wife's personality, her history, her feelings, her mind. Without even supervision to go to, in a strange kind of isolation where there was *no one* I could talk to about what I was hearing, I struggled to cope with what emerged. Gang-rape, sadism, murder, torture—these have not been stale concepts from second-hand experience. These have been lived out in front of me, in my lounge and in my bedroom, with a little one terrified at the punishment for spilling a drink, an inordinate terror that is impossible to disbelieve when you see someone you know so well switch to a different part of their personality and literally freeze in terror at something so innocuous.

It has changed my worldview. My sheltered upbringing did not prepare me for the scale of child abuse, the extent of organised abuse, or the big business of so-called "child pornography". I did not dream that there is so deep a seam of criminality in our world that exploits children to produce crude, sadistic images of abuse, that people collect these images as if they are stamps, that real, live children are raped and tortured to satisfy a coward's incorrigible and perverted lust. I was staggered by this knowledge.

At times the barrage of mental images conjured up by what I was hearing and seeing had a significant impact on my emotional state, causing high anxiety and sleep problems. Secondary traumatic stress—the way that someone else's trauma can infect your own psyche and mess with your head, just by being around it, just by witnessing it and smelling its stench—assaulted me repeatedly. It was so distressing to watch these alters, these parts that make up the totality of the woman who is *my wife*, reliving the abuse. And there was no escape from it—it happens at the tea-table, in bed, in the car. Therapists can try at least to partition off their life, seek supervision, and find solace in "normal" life. But this *was* normal life for me. I got to the point where I couldn't remember what it used to be like, before I knew about this stuff. I got to the point where I couldn't remember what it used to be like, when touch was easy and I never knew that respectable people from the middle classes intentionally planned and executed the repeated rapes and torture of infants and children. That sort of knowledge doesn't sit lightly in your head. It's not the kind of thing you can mention to your mates.

When at times we dared to be more open with people, the response was often upsetting. We found that the subject of child abuse, and certainly incest-based organised or ritualised abuse, is a step too far for most. Some listen politely. Some look shocked, verging on stunned. But most ask no questions and few if any ever mention it again. We found the dinner invites drying up, a tense but unspoken distance growing between us and our "friends". We had to learn to be wise, judging carefully who we thought would cope with our reality. We sadly realised that denial is a normative response to trauma, even someone else's, and it was easier for people to forget about our struggle than to face the realities of what had so devastated my wife.

I was unprepared at first for the backlash. People politely disappearing from our lives was one thing, but it astonished me to realise that so many people so vehemently deny the existence of dissociative disorders and the reality of extreme and organised abuse. About most things I am a conservative sceptic, but I experienced my wife's dissociation first and understood the label later. So when I began to read descriptions of what I was seeing, it all made perfect sense and it never occurred to me to doubt it. There is something viscerally real about observing for yourself your wife switch to a younger part of herself, relive a traumatic incident through visual and kinaesthetic and somatosensory flashbacks, and experience her lack of connected thinking and feeling and behaving. When I read descriptions of dissociation, like the American Psychiatric Association (2013) puts it, of "a disturbance of the integrative functions of identity, memory, or consciousness, and perception of the environment", then I laugh because it's so real. The definition feels stodgy, like all definitions do, but I know that it describes succinctly the reality I have seen of my wife in her adult self unable to connect to the memories, the feelings, the knowledge of herself as a child; and then my wife as her child self unable to draw on the cognitive understanding of the adult, that it's not her fault, that she's safe now, that it's over. That core lack of integration of knowledge and ability, of feelings and identity, of behaviour and meaning, is so evidently what I have seen since Carolyn's breakdown in 2005. And so it puzzles me that there is such a maelstrom of debate in some circles about the reality and existence of DID. *Come and spend a month with us*, I want to say. *Then you might believe it.*

Eventually, as enough of a narrative coalesced into words and there was sufficient emotional stability to build a platform from which to progress, we went to the police. It's not within everyone's power to do so. Many times I wish we hadn't. But Carolyn came to a place within herself, not where she needed the external validation of a successful prosecution to reassure her of her reality, but because she *was* convinced of her narrative: she knew that dangerous people were walking free, and she had no assurance that they weren't still doing to others what they had done to her. The step of reporting to the police in itself shattered our peace: more self-harm, more suicidality, prompted by the powerlessness of a situation in which communication is sparse and decision-making seemingly arbitrary. We had an initially positive experience of the police locally, who were convinced by Carolyn's rambling and disjointed account partly because it was so rambling and disjointed—it had none of the polish of a fabricated or confabulated account. She stuck to what she knew, which at times was frustratingly little—how do you trace a man from 30 years ago who was bald, or a youth with blonde hair, or a house with an upstairs bedroom? But there was enough to begin an investigation, and for the investigation to take sixteen months. The police corroborated dozens of details of Carolyn's story—buildings on farms in the exact layout she had described, places and people and visits and a chronology that was remarkably accurate given the extent of her previous amnesia. But not enough evidence to prosecute, so we were powerless once more.

But the smog that was our lives from 2005 onwards did begin to clear as the pollutants from Carolyn's childhood started to be processed. Gradually, control was restored: nights became for sleeping, days became steadier, more productive, and less volatile. Patterns were re-established of a working week, rhythms during each day. Carolyn continues to have therapy, describing it sometimes still as her "controlled explosion" where the un-integrations of her week are smelted together and given cohesive form. She continues to have DID, but her parts are more collaborative. They cooperate, they communicate, they enable Carolyn most of the time to live a productive and fruitful life. Night times can still be shattered by nightmares and pain. Somatic symptoms continue to plague her. She is not healed. That much trauma doesn't easily heal. But she is recovering. Her life has meaning and purpose.

If there is one thing that has characterised Carolyn's recovery to date, it has been her determination to succeed. Drummed into her through years of academic and sporting achievement, however out-of-control at times she was as she picked her way through the wreckage of her post traumatic and dissociative symptoms, she wasn't going to let it beat her. And she was going to change the world. That had always been our joke, even before the breakdown: we wanted to live our lives to change the world. So the business we briefly ran after we got married, the kids that we fostered, the social justice projects we were involved in: whatever we did, we wanted to change that little part of the world. It was never enough for Carolyn just to recover—she wanted others to recover too. And so it was that she first set up TASC (Trauma and Abuse Support Centre) in 2009, and together we set up PODS (Positive Outcomes for Dissociative Survivors) in 2010. We had to have learned something from our experiences that we could use to help others. The rejection and isolation, the sense of "insanity", the struggle for a sense of meaning, the descent towards divorce, the struggle with shame—somehow, we wanted and we still want to redeem our experiences and use them to help others. We do so imperfectly, but we do so passionately. PODS grew from supporting just a few partners in 2010 to an organisation at the start of 2012 with 2,000 people on the mailing list for its free e-magazine *Multiple Parts*. In 2011 Carolyn trained around 1,000 people.

I myself am training to be a therapist and I speak to dozens of people each month on the PODS helpline. It's good to be trying to help others; it's sad that there's such a need.

Carolyn's key message in all her writing and speaking is always hope. Sometimes I had to hold that hope for her. Sometimes she had to hold mine for me. At all times Carolyn's therapists held it for both of us. But the fact that our marriage has survived, the fact that Carolyn herself has survived, means that there is hope. Our lives haven't ever got back to normal. But strangely, I prefer the life we now have to the one we had before. I didn't sign up for being a partner of a dissociative survivor. I didn't think I could cope with that much stress, and that much heartache, and that much pain. But I did and I do. We are walking through this, into our new reality, together. Things will never get back to normal. But my wife is not mad. She's not making it all up. She's not attention-seeking. She's not psychotic. She is none of the things that dissociative survivors are so often accused of. She's just traumatised. And she's recovering.

And most importantly for me, she is still my wife.

Reference

American Psychiatric Association. (2013). *Diagnostic and Statistical Manual of Mental Disorders* (5th edn). Arlington, VA: APA.

CHAPTER TEN

Living well is the best revenge

Sue Bridger

I'm going to share with you a few of the ways I try to do just that.

I'm writing this as the free-flowing thoughts arise, more as if I were talking to you in a place that's comfortable for you. The language is simple so that my inner child (which is actually a mixture of many different child parts) can be included in the process. Your own inner child may help you to understand some of the things I say, so you might like to invite them to join you when you consider some of my suggestions.

Each person on a journey of recovery from childhood trauma will probably find, to a lesser or greater extent, that they have to navigate a path of their own making. But here are some things that I know have helped me, and if they do likewise for anyone else that would be wonderful. If not all of it is useful, then please, feel free to pick and choose, selecting any area of common ground and leaving the rest.

For the past dozen years or so I've been dealing with the uncovering of some very startling memories. At the same time I've had to cope with the recovery from associated trauma relating to this process of discovery—namely, the profound and chronic sexual and psychological abuse I experienced when I was very young. The person who was doing this to me was someone who I loved and depended on more than anyone else in the whole world, not only as a child but also throughout my entire life, up to and including recent years.

I had both denied this effectively to myself and fully known it, simultaneously, for five decades, and it is only recently that I have been able to work consciously through the full effects of this. The walls dividing the knowing from the denying parts of my mind seem thinner and more translucent as the light of a dawning awakening shines on, in and through, with an accompanying growing acceptance over time.

Comfort zones and windows of tolerance

It's been worth learning that I inhabit a comfort zone that's pretty small. Some people call this the "window of tolerance", and I like that name because windows can be nice and they bring air and light and a view beyond. They can bring hope with them, and also a possible opportunity of escape if it's needed. It's always good if I can return to this window of tolerance or comfort zone when I find myself slipping— either getting over-anxious or just "zoning out". It's like trying to adjust the clothing of my psyche so that I am comfortable between these two extremes.

"Take yourself to your safe place," my therapist used to say. The best therapists are the ones who don't pry too much into what my safe space looks like because I need this place to be just mine in order to *keep* it safe. I can be okay with telling general clues about what it feels like to *be* there, without giving too much away. It's the feelings of safety that it evokes which are the main thing, anyway, helping things to feel more on an even keel.

Solitude versus company

I have always found that I feel my most comfortable when I'm on my own. But if possible, I feel reassured by having a source of trusted support reasonably nearby, like knowing there is a good neighbour around, someone I can contact if I need to.

It makes an enormous difference to my wellbeing if I have a pet near me. This could be a hamster or a budgie or a dog or a cat … they are all effective because when an animal near me is calm, then that tells me, like a trusted barometer, that my world is safe. I trust their instincts and that means I don't have to feel so on edge and hyper-vigilant.

This has never worked so well with people, though: having another person in my space tends to be unnerving for me—even someone my mind would consider trustworthy. This might well have something to do with my automatic thoughts that I should have to respond to another person somehow, consider *their* needs rather than my own. Whatever the reason, I just don't breathe so easily as when I am on my own, and contact tends to become something I feel I have to endure rather than enjoy. So having enough solo time is very important to me, though it's important to watch the balance of this—if isolation slips in and replaces healthy solitude, that's not a helpful feeling. Maintaining contact time at an agreed length is helpful because the time boundary keeps me safe.

Toolkit

I do find that when I'm adventuring beyond my safety zone, it helps to have my imaginary toolkit with me. Even just taking a moment to tune into its existence really helps: *Is that bottle of Rescue Remedy still in my pocket?* Is everything as nice and simple as I can make it? I find if I get overloaded with things, then I get confused. *Have I got something to smell like that nice handcream, and what about those peppermints?* It's okay to take a hot water bottle with me in my bag if I want to, it's nice and reassuring to feel its warmth. *There's that lovely smooth pebble you've got, here it is in your pocket if you'd like something nice to touch. Have you got something to eat and to drink if you should need it?* I am like a caring mother packing for her child's day out. Actually, I'm not *like* one, I *am* one. I guess this is what re-parenting is all about, and I am continually learning how to do this with the gentleness, humour, love, and respect that the self-help books suggest. A lot of my recovery has been down to re-parenting myself. It's never too late to do that, especially when I have so many child parts living inside me who can enjoy feeling cared for so kindly.

Then there are the other things to put into the Mary Poppins toolbag: a prayer or a mantra to remember, and the very necessary and important present moment. Eckhart Tolle explains it very well in his book *The Power of Now*. It makes so much sense. I try to find a way to pack my breath in there too—now that *is* a hard one to remember! I have a tip I've found useful: to remind myself, as gently as possible, to breathe *out* before I breathe in. I have to let go of the old air to let the fresh air in.

Flashbacks and body memories

I also need to be prepared for those flashbacks and times when I feel like I'm under siege from haunting body-memories. I must remember that's what they are—memories, that's all. And I see it as a way of letting myself know that I'm processing all this. Just get out of the way, Sue, and let your system manage what it can do. Trust in the process, let the healing occur, and it will all come together in its own time.

I remember seeing a Babette Rothschild YouTube video about healing from trauma and it being compared to opening up a big bottle of fizzy drink that had been shaken. How do you do that, you may ask. The answer is s-l-o-w-l-y. We see the lid of the bottle being turned a bit at a time, and all the while there's a woman talking about it, and I'm watching and thinking it's all going to overflow and fizz everywhere … and it never does. I remember this at times of anxiety. That's my system working its way to recovery.

What's happening in the actual here and now? Can I get my "thinking brain" up and running? How many things in the room can I see that are red or green or beginning with the letter T? Remember that now I really am safe and okay, and repeatedly tell myself that. What sounds can I hear from outside the room? It's reassuring to remember there *are* good people in the world, including people I've never met. I can try to make a list of other people too; there are angels out there in human form who I don't even know of!

Dissociative parts

I find that my dissociative parts are more prone to come up when I'm feeling under some sort of threat, or if something's triggered me from the present into a past traumatic felt sense.

This seems to come with a sizzle of adrenaline, like a buzzy feeling, which can make me feel agitated, bring a sense of excitement and is often accompanied by a feeling of urgency. Strong wants and needs may come up suddenly. I may speak fast or use a different sort of vocabulary to usual. Concepts and words just aren't there to draw from in my head. I wave my hands a lot. I notice that I seem to be holding my head in an awkward position. My voice sounds different. Sometimes the furniture seems really big and the room looks different. Sometimes my mind seems to have disappeared, like it's just been whipped away.

I find it has been an enormous help for me to remind myself that I'm actually an adult woman now. I think that my inner child sometimes doesn't know this, or she needs reminding. I show her my feet and my size six shoes so she can see for herself. Or my hands—*They're grown-up hands, aren't they?* (In fact they're getting wrinkly.) Certainly not chubby pink and sweaty like they used to be when I was little. I show her my home and reassure her that it's not the place she was when things were horrid. I am convinced she listens and looks with wonder with her big child eyes through my adult ones in the present when I show her this.

Another discovery was just how effective it can be to tell my inner child that I am going to have to do something that I have to do alone as an adult, and that she had best go and find a safe place to play. This is particularly useful to remember to do when I go to a place or see a person and I could get triggered into flashbacks. I may have to repeat this when I get out of the car, encouraging little Sue to stay there, do some colouring-in, or look at some nice books. I tell her I'll be back soon, and always try to remember to return with lots of praise and thanks for allowing me to do what I alone had to do.

Keep safe now

I try to keep myself as safe as I can in my world today. I look after my physical wellbeing and try to watch whether I can do anything to make myself feel better. Am I Hungry, Angry, Lonely, or Tired? HALT if so, and take action to make things better! *Best not make commitments to do more than you think you are able, Sue. Now's the time to look after yourself, isn't it—to focus on things that contribute to your own wellbeing. And hey, do your best to avoid those people, places, and things that don't do this.* Don't force myself to do the social things I find a strain. Be kind to myself. Give back to myself the compassion I need; this will also aid my recovery, so the experts say.

Therapy

In therapy I need to work in a way that's as safe for me as possible, or else it feels like I'm going to blow a gasket. The connection, the relationship that I have with the therapist, is the all-important thing for me. If I come to you for therapy then please don't give me false presentations of yourself: I'm used to reading people, I've done it since I was very small, so I can read through all that. It's a part of my make-up to have antennae, after all. When or if you pretend, you are only making yourself untrustworthy to me. How can I possibly be honest with you if I don't trust you? And how can I get better if I am not honest?

The therapist has to be aware that although it may look like they're talking to a grown-up, there are actually several different children and teenage and other grown-up parts who may be there too. Did you know that these can hear you when you speak to them? The little ones love it when you talk kindly to me, using words that they can understand. Could you maybe support me in trying to get a good relationship going between my own adult and my child parts? Help me re-parent myself with loving kindness and the good care I so need? Please understand that it's better for me to get to depend on myself than on you or anyone else, because I am the only one with me all of the time, and it's scary for me to rely on someone else in case they disappear.

What didn't help me feel better was going to groups or one-to-one therapy where I was encouraged to revisit the past with the protection of some guardian figure. This didn't work for me whether I was accompanied by my adult self, Jesus, Buddha, Superwoman, or any angelic being, whether they were beside me, above me, around me, or within me. What tended to happen was that any trauma just got re-triggered and I was left feeling that I didn't pray the right way or believe in the right way, or couldn't love in the right way or do a therapeutic exercise the right way. Once again, there was something wrong with *me*.

So please don't try to take me back to the trauma memories, because they hurt me too much and I need a break from them anyway. Could you perhaps help me find some superpowers to visualise that can help to keep me safe now, please? That'd be better. I so need to feel okay *now*.

Can I try to make sure I give myself the attention and care that I need? I've managed to cut myself off pretty effectively from my needs. Do I have any? What are they? Now I fully realise that much of my recovery *depends* on me seeing myself as worthy of good, of happiness, of peace, of respect, of living life the way that I choose to, and discerning what my needs are and responding to them.

My inner checker

I need lots of reassurance that things are okay—*Yes, the door is locked.* I have a very rigorous door checker part who likes to do her job often and well. Is the fear in real time or is it in memory? Whatever, it must be done. I give her thanks. Can I detect her somewhat glowing with pride when I do that? She's glad to be of service. She goes on telling me to recheck and sometimes I've had to do it just to reassure her. I will try to tell her at the same time—*See? it's okay, really it is. We're safely locked and the key is nearby in case we want to get out in a hurry for any reason. It's okay, we're safe now.*

I think my door checker part has another role, which is to keep the bathroom clean. She does like to make sure it's okay and fit for a queen! The same sense of pride and satisfaction comes to me when she has the bathroom under control as when the door is safely locked. Again, thanks and praise given.

Reassurance

Even after the nightmares or the flashbacks I try to remind myself that it's all OK. *This happens when you're dealing with such big stuff, Sue. And that's what you're doing. You've gone through such a big shock in realising the past was how it was. Be nice and gentle with yourself. It's all OK. Can you feel your feet on the floor? Can you lengthen your spine, because that makes you feel more grown-up and stronger? Do you feel a bit better now? You're doing really well. What do you need just now? Can big Sue look after all the little Sues that exist inside?*

It can feel like repeatedly fighting an enemy that's attacking not only from outside but also from within. Can I try to turn the inner demons into my friends who only want to help me in their own way? Can we try to be all on the same team and work together?

Go with the process, it's all right. Just breathe. The only way out of the tunnel when you've started to crawl inside it, is through. When you're going through hell, keep going. Trust the process. You're doing really well. You will get there.

I give as much reassurance to myself as possible.

Feelings

For many years I had no tears, especially at the beginning of the memories and when dissociation was playing a strong part. Came off antidepressants for a while thinking this would help me contact my emotions but no, all I felt was depression, not emotion. When any tearful sensation might arise now, I welcome it and the spirit that comes with it. There's some kind of a connection that's real and deep and true. It's still a very rare thing so when it comes up it's a real gem. There's something about feeling in touch with my vulnerability which I experience as, surprisingly, quite beautiful.

Maybe I'd spent such a lot of time protecting myself from feelings that were bad I'd ended up doing a "sweep" job of screening myself from feelings altogether. I guess it really is true that we cannot selectively numb emotion. When we numb hard feelings they say we can't do so without also numbing joy, happiness, or even a sense of vulnerability that can connect me with a beautiful and tender part of myself, a certain exquisiteness. When that happens I get a glimpse of me being in sync with the whole of me, being authentic, courageous, and true.

When I get the chance to see, to meet, my vulnerability it feels like I'm also dropping the masks that, like everyone, I can get all too attached to wearing—the parts of me that believe I should be doing such and such, or behaving in such a way. It can be seen as a letting go of the "shoulds" in order to be who I really am.

It takes courage, but it's worth wearing this badge of authenticity as a part of my battledress to touch on wholeness and truth in my being. "The wound is the place where the light enters you," says Rumi the mystic; and so does Leonard Cohen: "There is a crack, a crack in everything/That's how the light gets in." Is there any connection between the word *blesser*, "to wound" in French, and me being "blessed" by having these wounds? Perhaps not, but can I look at it as if there is? Could it be true that reaching a time when I want to face the feelings instead of flee from them is a sign of integration and health, an advance from the stage of feeling blitzed and blown apart?

Companions

When I am in contact with others the best people are those who can look after and take responsibility for themselves. That's not at all to say that it's not good to hear my friends speak about their stuff, it's just that as a recovering adult-child I do not need to feel I have to be *responsible* for anyone except myself. I just can't *do* that when I need every single hand on deck that I've got, to look after myself and all the different parts I have within.

Other good folk to have as contacts and friends are those who are also in touch with their own inner child. Some things, I've found, can be best understood by another surviving adult-child working through their own childhood trauma. Maybe that's what we're all doing to a greater or lesser extent?

Acceptance

Acceptance of dissociation as a part of my reality was a huge step towards recovery. Acceptance of this and the reason for it being there is very important too. Another thing that helped enormously with the healing, when I finally could do it, was giving myself permission not to see the abuser any more. Up till then, while contact was still taking place, it was a bit like driving a car with the brake and the accelerator pressed down at the same time.

It also helped to recognise that things might have to get worse before they got better. When this happened, and I did actually feel worse, trying to see it as part of the recovery process, and therefore a *good* sign, was the way round it.

Giving as much kindness and compassion as possible back to me is always important, even towards the parts that are not so nice. In fact it was a great help when I could take on board and accept that the "bad" voices were a part of me as well as the nicer ones. Somehow they became nicer when met with an understanding that they were trying in their own way to help me. My aim is to try to get us all working on the same team, and it's actually beginning to feel like that's what we're starting to do.

Self-harm

A part of me does think that the answer is to self-harm. This thought can give me some sense of power over feeling that I am helpless and without any control over anything, and that, along with accompanying feelings of soothing and numbing that arise when self-harming, can fool me into thinking this is a good choice. This is always a tough one: paradoxically, sometimes *not* to self-harm can actually feel like it's going against actually *helping* yourself. Distraction from the thought can be a help here and I can suggest to myself, *Well, just for now I won't do that, and I can get occupied doing something else.*

The more the practice of self-care gets to be the favoured option, the less the self-harmer makes her suggestions. I see her as a misguided friend offering solutions that aren't going to be right for me.

What helped me with this difficult subject was the clear notion that it would be adding on extra time to my overall recovery if I did this, and all for the sake of feeling a momentary relief.

Freeing up space

Getting rid of things around me that don't make me feel good is always a great idea. If a part of me feels attached to an object that I know isn't making me feel good to have around, then it can feel easier to part with if I take a photo of it before dropping it off at the charity shop.

My home has to be safest of safe. *Especially* my bedroom. And as clear as possible of muddle and mess.

A few tips

These things work for me:

- Not answering the phone or the door unless really wanting to was such a relief once I had given myself permission to do it.
- Sticking up on noticeboards or walls inspiring pictures, quotes, and sayings that would get replaced by other feel-good items once they stopped having an effect. Surrounding myself with healing and nice things that make me feel good.
- Trying to soak the good feelings up into the very cells of my body, my entire being.
- Allowing myself to get absorbed and thrilled by programmes on CBBC. *Not* the re-runs of Sooty and Bill and Ben from my childhood but newer programmes like *In the Night Garden* or *Teletubbies*.
- Feeding my inner children's delight in going round toyshops. Reading children's books. Different-aged child parts like different kinds of books—I can negotiate with them the ones they want to see and the ones they don't like.
- Giving little presents that delight my inner child. Asking the shop assistant to giftwrap the item delights my inner child all the more.
- Buying a special doll that represents me as a child that I work hard at giving love to—it's taking time but I am getting there.
- Pottering/playing in the garden—sitting on the ground using a trowel.

- Allowing myself to get muddy hands. Planting bulbs. Making little dens in the garden "for the fairies"!
- Talking to the dog, to the trees, to the birds. Singing—my inner child loves to sing!
- Writing letters from and to my child parts—especially helpful to read what I write back to myself from "my wise part".

The clever mind

To acknowledge that abominable atrocities of unspeakable things happened to me when I was very little and defenceless is frankly enough to help me accept that all the strange behaviour was actually the cleverness of my spirit protecting myself. Yes, I managed by incorporating some kind of complex "double-think"—simultaneously knowing and denying. It was a very *clever* way of getting by with the appalling reality of the truth that has only just begun to get attention.

The journey continues

I know there are different parts of who I am. The whole range of feelings, moods, wishes, or emotional states I experience could originate from any one of those parts. The parts do not act in cooperation with each other: when one's in operation, she doesn't feel like a *part*. She *may* just be a part but she *feels* like she takes up a *whole* space.

But inside, there's also a wise me who is connected to a bigger and higher power, who I know and trust can work towards getting me better and connect my life with health and wholeness. I trust and I believe in this. I recognise the utter importance of reclaiming my own hurt child and making sure I do my best to protect her from now on. I have a commitment of care to my inner child and she loves it when I tell her this.

Reference

Tolle, E. (2001). *The Power of Now*. London: Hodder.

CHAPTER ELEVEN

Medical aspects of recognising complex dissociative disorders

Ruth Cureton

There is no division between body and mind. Those people suffering from stress related illness develop a range of demonstrable physical pathologies more often than the general population and those who suffer from long-term physical illnesses also tend to suffer from a range of psychological symptoms. It is in my view this artificial distinction which leads to so much stigmatisation in psychiatry.

—Dr Tim Cantopher FRCPsych (2007)

It is towards the end of a Friday afternoon surgery and an overstretched GP is considering management plans for palpitations, severe episodic headaches, abdominal pains precipitating collapse, debilitating joint pains, insomnia, unexplained vaginal bleeding, and memory difficulties; and all in the same patient.

To whom can the GP refer such a patient? What tests and investigations might help with diagnosis? Even if the GP senses that many of the patient's symptoms and day-to-day difficulties may be consequences of unresolved trauma and stress, each symptom and sign (as revealed on examination) has to be considered for diagnostic assessment and possible referral on to various hospital specialists. And to be frank, the hospital model is largely geared towards bodily systems going wrong one at a time, rather than looking for overarching causality.

The long-term consequences of chronic, severe childhood trauma and abuse, particularly against a background of disorganised attachment, can be many and varied, impacting on a survivor's development both physiologically and psychologically, not to mention relationally, emotionally, and spiritually. At some point in their lives survivors may find themselves in a crisis of "perfect storm" proportions, despite having functioned reasonably well through years, or even decades, of childhood, adolescence, and adulthood.

All this can be extremely distressing and disorienting for the survivor and their friends and family, as well as challenging and perplexing for health professionals. More recent developments in the fields of attachment, trauma recovery, and dissociation have made a great deal of sense of otherwise confusingly complex symptomatology (Steinberg & Schnall, 2000).

Are complex dissociative disorders treatable?

A frequent objection is that complex dissociative disorders are too difficult to treat and too draining on health resources. This is patently not so: "Of disorders of comparable severity, dissociative disorders are very responsive to talk therapies" (Sidran Traumatic Stress Foundation, 2010).

The Treatment of Patients with Dissociative Disorders (TOP DD) study, based at Towson University, Maryland USA, recruited about 290 therapists and their clients from eighteen countries, making it the largest and only international study of dissociative disorders. The study has shown improvement over a range of parameters, with further publication of results yet to come (see www.towson.edu/topddstudy/publications.asp for TOP DD publications).

An article in the *Health Service Journal* (Lloyd, 2011) describes how investing in therapy can produce overall cost savings to the NHS: that is, that one-to-one psychotherapy can be cost-effective for DID.

An unpublished single case study shows how establishing psychotherapy can bring about massive savings in inpatient and outpatient costs (Sidran Institute 2010):

> Treatment generally takes over seven years from diagnosis for a female survivor with DID.

What is dissociation?

Dissociation is an involuntary psychological separation of awareness of perceptions that are usually associated together, such as time, place, thoughts, feelings, memories, and identity. There are a range of causes and degrees of severity.

Severe dissociation is usually caused by traumatisation, when a person's coping mechanisms are overwhelmed and set off instinctive survival responses. Where the survival responses of fight, flight, or freeze are ineffective or unavailable, and the threat (whether real or perceived) persists, then submit and/or collapse responses may follow, sometimes including marked dissociation. Most people at the severe end of the dissociative spectrum, living with Dissociative Identity Disorder (DID) or Dissociative Disorder Not Otherwise Specified (DDNOS), have suffered severe, ongoing, and often organised criminal trauma and abuse in childhood, against a background of disorganised attachment (Hatloy, 2013).

What part does disorganised attachment play?

A child's growing attachment to parent figures is crucial to every aspect of development. It is during interactions with attachment figures that the nervous system is nourished and developed. The starkest evidence for this is seen in globally neglected Romanian orphans, where MRI scans of the brain show large areas of non-development. These children may present as unattached to any parental or other figure (Schore, 2003).

Disorganised attachment patterns may develop when parent figures are experienced as frightening and/or frightened, meaning that the child's supposed sources of comfort and safety are dangerous, ill-equipped to protect the growing child, or both. This makes the processing of, and recovery from, traumas that occur during childhood extremely difficult, whether or not the parent figure(s) are the direct cause of those traumas. The adverse events or abuses are left in a raw and unprocessed state, often deep within the child's psyche.

Neglect of attachment needs in childhood, accompanied by severe, chronic trauma and/or any form of physical, sexual, or psychological abuse, particularly where the perpetrators are attachment figures, may lead to increasingly complex post-traumatic stress, with marked fragmentation of the developing child's sense of identity and narrative, and compartmentalisation of experiences. For example, the "part" of the child that attends school during the day may be completely unaware of the incestuous abuse occurring during the night. Such knowledge would be intolerable, rendering the child unable to function in other ways that may be essential to keeping the compliance and silence demanded of them. Hence dissociation works as a survival mechanism that enables the child's sanity and day-to-day functioning to remain intact, especially in the ongoing presence of one or more perpetrators.

Why do symptoms of post-traumatic stress occur?

When the traumatisation is severe and recurring the nervous system remains constantly on hyper-alert, with the cortex frequently bypassed. This is characterised by chronically high levels of cortisol circulating, somatic symptoms, generalised anxiety, marked startle reflex, mood swings, and unpredictable responses to environmental stimuli.

Within the triune brain (the brain stem, limbic system, and cortex), functions of daily life are governed at three levels:

1. Automatically, such as the heart beating, in the subcortical brain stem
2. Instinctively, such as turning away from a foul smell, in the subcortical limbic system
3. After thought and consideration, such as deciding what clothes to wear, cortically.

Survival mechanisms kick in when a person is under real or perceived threat. Once the internal alarm is raised, the cortex is bypassed for expediency. For example: when walking into a road and seeing a car coming, a person "instinctively" steps back on the pavement (mediated subcortically via the limbic system and brain stem); when the immediate threat has passed and the cortex is back online, the person can think about the incident, processing new learning to check the road more carefully before stepping out again.

Under the age of around three, or whenever on "red alert", memory is stored via the limbic amygdala ("Am I in danger?"); that is, it is subcortically mediated. Smells, sounds, sights, bodily sensations, and experienced emotions stored via the amygdala are not easily connected to cortical cognitions and learning. This is true both of events occurring at an early age and when the cortex is bypassed during a traumatic event.

Increasingly, from around age three onwards and during non-traumatic experiences, memories are stored via the hippocampus ("huge filing cabinet") and are cortically processed. These memories are stored sequentially, along with time, place, person, thoughts, and outcome, and are much more easily retrieved and connected to cognitions for processing and learning.

A person with a background of abuse and/or trauma may suffer from intrusions such as flashbacks, as well as being susceptible to reminders or triggers. Triggering occurs when one or more smells, sounds, sights, situations, persons, emotions, or fragments of memory make a sudden and unexpected connection with a pocket of, usually amygdala-mediated, emotionally loaded, not yet processed, feelings and sensations.

These memories were not stored sequentially via the hippocampus precisely because they were too overwhelming to be integrated at the time. This precipitates a "red alert" limbic amygdala-mediated response; the cortex is bypassed because of the perceived threat, and the arousal level moves far beyond the usual "window of tolerance" (optimal arousal zone) with unpredictable consequences often resulting in re-traumatisation.

When survivors are in their window of tolerance—that is, when arousal/stress levels are manageable and the cortex is fully available for processing memories and useful learning—then cognitive and behavioural approaches may be learnt and absorbed effectively enough to be useful in later management of symptoms.

However, when a survivor is in a state of hyperarousal, on "red alert" and taken up with fight, flight, or freeze responses, cognitive approaches are unlikely to be effective, because the cortex is not fully functioning. In this state a person may present with rigid posture, agitation, restlessness, tearfulness, and/or anger.

Conversely, in a state of hypoarousal a person may present as defeated and in a state of collapse. These are submit or collapse responses, where a person is "boiled over and switched off". A person may appear as literally collapsed, with flaccid posture, withdrawn, zoned out, and mute. Severe dissociative episodes are most likely to occur during a period of hypoarousal (Ogden, Minton & Pain, 2006).

Challenges faced by survivors with DID or DDNOS

On a day-to-day basis, and taking a massive toll on their general health, wellbeing, relationships, and future prospects, survivors face specific symptoms such as dissociative amnesia/fugue, dissociative stupor/ collapse, anaesthesia and sensory loss, muscle and movement disorders, dissociative convulsions, depersonalisation, and derealisation.

Common comorbidities with complex dissociative disorders include anxiety and depression; attachment disorders—attention-seeking and/or avoidant patterns; somatisation disorders—complex, chronic systemic pain and fatigue; illusions and hallucinations (though full blown delusions are unusual); intrusions—flashbacks, triggering, panic attacks, sleep disorders; and avoidances—phobia, agoraphobia, pronounced reaction to current day traumas.

Also, when a complex dissociative disorder is the primary diagnosis, various behavioural strategies may partly offset chronic anxiety, such as obsessive-compulsive behaviours, risk-taking behaviours, addictive behaviours, eating disorders, and self-harm and suicidality.

These addictive-type behaviours are unconsciously employed as partial solutions to the profound unresolved internal, and often external, conflicts that are part and parcel of living with complex dissociative disorders.

An addiction can be defined as "any set of behaviours which an individual employs to attempt to deal with negative feelings, which then get out of control causing the feelings to get worse and therefore needing more of the behaviours" (Cantopher, 2012).

Behavioural coping mechanisms are themselves widely misunderstood. They are functioning as "partial solutions", which is why they're so habit-forming and hard to move on from. This is over and above any physical dependency.

But if a person is barely managing to stop themselves from drowning by holding on to a bit of flotsam, then what's needed is a non-judgemental context to consider a safe enough alternative "lifeboat" before we can expect them to let the flotsam go. This myriad of symptoms and disorders mean that survivors face isolation, misunderstanding, and misdiagnosis.

It is crucial to support the survivor in exploring less damaging options for managing their intense emotions and profound feelings of isolation, hopelessness, powerlessness, and voicelessness. Making any therapeutic contact conditional on changes in the survivor's behaviour, or seeking to forcibly stop these partial solutions, may precipitate even more drastic coping mechanisms and behaviours.

Why is specialist assessment and diagnosis so often delayed?

I have talked with many survivors living with complex dissociative disorders who are extraordinarily appreciative of the treatment they are receiving as they work towards recovery. What I find incredibly challenging is the length of time, running into years, it has often taken them to get access to specialised treatment (2011, Lloyd M.).

Various factors contribute to delays in the process of presentation, diagnosis, and treatment.

The stigma associated with psychological and psychosomatic disorders

One of biggest barriers to survivors asking for help in the first place is the stigma and shame associated with having psychological and psychosomatic disorders.

As a GP I was more than willing to treat other people facing such health challenges with understanding and empathy, yet when my own health began to fail I put off seeking help until the situation was very severe, because I was ashamed of having psychological difficulties, and feared that it would affect how colleagues and others viewed me in the future.

Consider for a moment some other long-term health problems: polio infection in childhood may leave someone permanently disabled; severe kidney infections may result in needing renal dialysis later in life; brain damage in a car accident may limit a child's future development. Should any of these conditions carry a stigma and leave the child, or later the adult, feeling toxic levels of shame? No one asks: "Why did you breathe in the polio germs?" or "Why didn't you look after your kidneys better?" or "Why did you get in the car when your father told you to?" There may or may not be culpable adults involved, yet one intuitively knows the child to be innocent in each case.

So why is it that adult survivors presenting with the untreated sequelae of childhood neglect, trauma, and abuse not only feel deeply ashamed, but are frequently shamed still further by being told to "pull yourself together", "forget it and get on with your life", or "just stop thinking about it"? Does anyone seriously doubt that the vast majority of survivors would gladly forget it all and get on with a contented ful-filled life now, if only that were possible?

Consider the wide range of difficulties survivors may be battling with:

- specific dissociative symptomatology, such as dissociative amnesia
- the intrusions, avoidances, hypervigilance, and anxiety of PTSD
- behavioural adaptations, such as eating disorders or addictive behaviours
- the developmental consequences of lacking a secure childhood base
- impact on education, employment, and future prospects
- the long-term impact on relationships and social skills
- sequelae of bodily damage that occurred in childhood
- somatisation disorders and other comorbidities.

First consider the above consequences in relation to a ten-year-old child. Who would deny such a child a full and thorough specialist assessment of needs and a multidisciplinary care plan?

Now consider the same consequences in relation to a forty-year-old parent of growing children, who is unable to work due to intractable PTSD and other symptoms? I see no possible justification for the adult not receiving the same level of specialist assessment and care as the child, particularly when there is growing evidence of the cost savings to the NHS over time of providing such treatments (Lloyd, 2011).

The complexity of presentation

Complex dissociative disorders including DID and DDNOS are now widely understood as complex forms of post-traumatic stress disor-der, where some combination of severe neglect, trauma, and abuse has occurred in childhood, against a background of disorganised attach-ment and across a child's developmental stages.

The very complexities that make these disorders so challenging to live with also pose major diagnostic challenges, particularly when health services generally assume that patients will have problems with one organ, or one bodily system, at any one time.

Specialists are highly trained is their own areas but their role is not generally to take an overview of the patient's wellbeing, though services for children and the elderly do operate more holistically. The path to diagnosis may prove tortuous for both doctor and patient, particularly if medical examinations, tests, and treatments are experienced as invasive and re-traumatising for the survivor.

Mental health services usually operate a multidisciplinary team approach but seem seriously under-resourced in relation to non-psychotic mental health issues and disorders.

The complex, long-term consequences of severe ongoing neglect, trauma, and abuse in childhood are yet to be fully grasped and addressed by the survivors themselves, their friends and family, health professionals, and indeed by the wider community. This leaves countless survivors with an untold burden of treatable ill health, impacting them, their loved ones, and their prospects for a thriving healthy future (Aquarone & Hughes, 2006).

Rapid developments in the fields of attachment and trauma recovery

The most prolific incidences of PTSD tend to occur in relation to war. Consider these scenarios:

- World War I: some whose shell shock rendered them incapable of fighting were regarded as cowards or deserters and sentenced to death by firing squad.
- World War II: awareness of battle fatigue with fugue states and other trauma-related symptoms was emerging, with military hospitals providing a refuge for some.
- Falklands war: increasing understanding and awareness of PTSD, though treatment programmes were still in the early stages of development.
- Afghanistan war: PTSD is now understood and effective treatments are available, though provision of services may still be scarce and variable.

So why do we hear time and again from adult survivors with complex dissociative disorders who report denial of the validity of their trauma-related symptoms; misdiagnosis with other conditions, such as psychotic episodes, bipolar disorders, personality disorders, or even factitious conditions; delays in accessing specialist assessment and diagnosis; refusal of funding for a full diagnostic assessment with health professionals specialising in complex dissociative disorders; and refusal of funding for specialist treatment?

I recently heard a personal anecdote regarding a patient incarcerated in a mental health unit (not in the UK) for over forty years, before finally beginning specific trauma recovery therapy in the 1990s. The patient described how their psychiatric diagnosis had evolved over the decades. On initial admission in the 1960s the diagnosis was paranoid schizophrenia. A decade or so later the predominant opinion was that the primary condition was manic depression (now bipolar disorder). Another ten years passed and by then the considered opinion was that the patient was suffering from borderline personality disorder, for which no treatment was available at the time. This series of changes in diagnosis may seem bizarre to the contemporary observer, but actually testifies to the rapid rate of progress in the mental health field over recent decades, both in trauma recovery and the role of attachment disorders in adults.

What cannot be justified is that survivors with complex dissociative disorders are still to this day being misdiagnosed with psychoses, bipolar disorder, or borderline personality disorder. While some survivors may have such co-morbid conditions, the possible role and sequelae of childhood neglect, trauma, and abuse should always be considered, precisely because effective treatments now exist.

All mental health disorders should receive the best available diagnostic assessments and the most effective treatments and support services. However, my work in the charitable sector of this particular field has indicated that there are undoubtedly large numbers of survivors in the UK (certainly hundreds, possibly thousands or even more) who have treatable psychological disorders, such as DDNOS or DID, who have not had specialist assessment and are not receiving ideal treatment, or in some cases not receiving any treatment at all.

The challenge of coding diagnoses in a rapidly developing field

Correct initial diagnosis is crucial if survivors are to receive the most appropriate treatment from health professionals with specialised training and experience. Trauma recovery, attachment disorders in adults, and complex dissociative disorders are not yet part of the standard initial training for many health professions, nor automatically included in their continuing professional development. There are centres of excellence but provision is patchy and resources scarce.

This situation is aggravated by the developing systems for coding diagnoses. With the now widespread dependence on electronic information and transmission systems, computer coding for these particular disorders is crucial to development of UK treatment guidelines through the National Institute for Health and Care Excellence (NICE); to communication between health professionals; to the survivor's own understanding of, and engagement with, treatment and care plans, and for communication between their supporters and other health professionals involved.

Coding diagnosis is complex in the UK, with four main systems:

- **ICD-10** (International Classification of Diseases, 10th revision, including the Classification of Mental and Behavioural Disorders; WHO, 1994) is used most commonly by doctors in the UK.
- **DSM-5** (Diagnostic and Statistical Manual of Mental Disorders, fifth edition; APA, 2013) is the USA standard, more often used in research in the UK.
- **Read Codes** are clinical terms used to record patient findings and procedures in health and social care IT systems across primary and secondary care.
- **SNOMED CT** (Systematized Nomenclature of Medicine—Clinical Terms) is the most comprehensive clinical healthcare terminology in the world, to which the NHS is gradually moving.

Looking in more detail at the classification of complex dissociative disorders in ICD-10, the main groups of disorder are:

- Organic, including symptomatic, mental disorders such as dementia
- Mental and behavioural disorders due to psychoactive substance use
- Schizophrenia, schizotypal, and delusional disorders
- Mood (affective) disorders, such as manic, bipolar, or depressive episodes
- Behavioural syndromes associated with physiological disturbances, for example eating disorders

- **Neurotic, stress-related, and somatoform disorders**
- Developmental and childhood disorders and so on, such as attachment disorders.

Neurotic, stress-related and somatoform disorders further subdivides into:

- Phobic anxiety disorders
- Agoraphobia
- Social phobias
- Specific (isolated) phobias
- Panic disorder (episodic paroxysmal anxiety)
- Generalised anxiety disorder, that is, it is "free-floating"
- Mixed anxiety and depressive disorder
- Obsessive-compulsive disorders
- Reaction to severe stress and adjustment disorders
- ***Acute stress reaction**
- ****Post-traumatic stress disorder**
- **Dissociative (conversion) disorders**, previously classified as various types of "conversion hysteria". Medical examination and investigation do not reveal the presence of any known physical or neurological disorder; includes reaction hysteria
- **Dissociative amnesia**
- **Dissociative fugue**
- **Dissociative stupor**—profound diminution or absence of voluntary movement and normal responsiveness
- **Trance and possession disorders**—temporary loss of the sense of identity and full awareness of the surroundings
- **Dissociative motor disorders**—loss of ability to move the whole or a part of the limbs or loss of speech
- **Dissociative convulsions**—closely mimic epileptic seizures but tongue-biting, bruising, and incontinence are rare
- **Dissociative anaesthesia and sensory loss**—anaesthetic areas of skin are associated with the patient's ideas rather than with medical knowledge
- **Mixed and other dissociative (conversion) disorders**—Ganser syndrome
- *****Multiple personality**—psychogenic

- **Somatoform disorders**—repeated physical symptoms and requests for medical investigations; no physical basis
- **Somatisation disorder**—frequently changing physical symptoms; long and complicated history of negative investigations. Excludes malingering
- **Hypochondriacal disorder**
- **Somatoform autonomic dysfunction**
- **Depersonalisation-derealisation syndrome**—a rare disorder in which mental activity, body, and surroundings change their quality, so as to be unreal, remote, or automatised; most frequently loss of emotions and feelings of estrangement or detachment from their thinking, their body, or the real world.

Many survivors and health professionals will recognise the following description:

*Acute stress reaction (crisis state; psychic shock)

A transient disorder that develops in response to exceptional physical and mental stress and that usually subsides within hours or days.

The symptoms show a typically mixed and changing picture and include an initial state of "daze", inability to comprehend, and disorientation. This state may be followed either by further withdrawal from the surrounding situation (dissociative stupor) or by agitation and over-activity (flight reaction). Signs of panic (tachycardia, sweating, flushing) are commonly present. The symptoms usually appear within minutes of the impact of the stressful stimulus or event, and disappear within two to three days. There may be partial or complete amnesia for the episode. (ICD-10, 1994)

**Post-Traumatic Stress Disorder includes a number of the core symptoms experienced in complex dissociative disorders:

Long-lasting response to a stressful event or situation of an exceptionally threatening or catastrophic nature, which is likely to cause pervasive distress in almost anyone. Predisposing factors, such as personality traits, previous illness, may make it more likely.

Intrusions: reliving of the trauma in intrusive memories (flashbacks), dreams, nightmares, hypervigilance, startle reactions, and insomnia.

Avoidances: of activities and situations reminiscent of the trauma, persisting sense of numbness and emotional blunting, unresponsiveness to surroundings and detachment from other people.

Anxiety and depression are commonly associated with the above symptoms, and suicidal ideation is not infrequent. The onset follows the trauma with a latency period that may range from a few weeks to months or years. The course is fluctuating but recovery can be expected in the majority of cases.

In a small proportion of cases the condition may follow a chronic course over many years. (ICD-10, 1994)

DID and DDNOS are listed as such in DSM-IV but not in ICD-10, where the old terminology is still used:

> **Mixed and other dissociative (conversion) disorders**—*Ganser syndrome*
> ***Multiple personality**—*psychogenic*

The diagnoses at the top of the Neurotic, stress-related and somatoform disorders, such as agoraphobia and OCD, have gradually gained recognition and effective treatments have been developed; further down the list the descriptive language becomes more challenging and unhelpful.

This is partly because psychological disorders are so difficult to quantify and monitor. Consider, for example, thyroid gland disorders, which can usually be accurately assessed via a series of blood tests. Then compare psychological disturbances, which are affected by a multitude of factors, such as: levels of neurotransmitters in the brain and nervous system; countless electrical impulses continuously passing to and fro between the brain and every other part of the body; many complex feedback and auto-regulatory systems governed by our brain, endocrine glands and other organs; the levels of vitamins and trace elements in our body tissues and bloodstream; food and fluids we have ingested; medicines, drugs, and chemicals we consume; not to mention interactions with our family, friends, colleagues, strangers, media, and the weather!

The unhelpfulness of the language of ICD-10 has its origins in the artificial distinction between the brain and the body, the *psyche* and the *soma* in Latin, from which the term psychosomatic is derived. In the past there has been a widespread assumption that psychological factors in health are under voluntary, conscious control, implying that psychosomatic conditions are somehow less worthy of medical attention.

But is the driven workaholic executive who presents at A&E with a bleeding duodenal ulcer told to "pull yourself together"? Is the grieving widower who has a heart attack three months after his wife's death told to "stop thinking about her and you'll get over it"? Of course not, it would be scandalous to blame the patient in either of these scenarios for their own medical emergencies. Yet a value judgement is all too often made when a trauma survivor, whilst overwhelmed by seemingly insoluble distress, has harmed themselves. All too many survivors report profoundly re-traumatising experiences at the hands of health professionals from whom they ought, at the very least, to be able to expect an objective, non-judgemental response.

One of my favourite quotes about psychosomatic disorders is actually in a novel about the origins of psychiatry, set in the 1890s, with characters such as Sigmund Freud and Pierre Janet as contemporaries of the fictional doctor Jacques who describes his work with "hysterical" patients:

> I had wanted to call [my work] "Psychosomatic Resolution", but it has been pointed out that many people do not understand this … It truly means "existing in mind and body", and is often used of physical symptoms whose cause is in the mind; it suggests a "double existence" … but a common misunderstanding has it as little more than a synonym for "imagined"; that in many people's minds, far from meaning "dually existent" or "doubly real", it means unreal or non-existent! (Faulks, 2008)

Neuroscience, in particular research using functional MRI scanning, has shown beyond doubt that our minds and bodies are inextricably and profoundly linked, with feedback loops throughout our nervous system, along with "somatic", that is, bodily storage of memories. So someone who was, for example, punched and kicked during a mugging, may find that they can still "feel" the blows months or even years after the event, particularly when triggering reminders of the traumatic event arise.

MRI studies also show that the hippocampus ("huge filing cabinet") area of the brain is smaller in survivors of chronic trauma, and then increases in size during therapy—an indication, perhaps, of how much trauma was still left "unprocessed" and raw. Functional MRI studies are clearly demonstrating different patterns of reaction in areas of the brain in those with varying degrees of trauma (Hopper, Frewen, van der Kolk, & Lanius, 2007).

Chronic trauma has an impact on our whole systems—neurotransmitters, hormones, immunity, and physical, emotional, and spiritual health. There is absolutely no doubt in my mind that responses to disorganised attachment, neglect, trauma, and abuse are physiological, that is, bodily, despite being difficult to quantify and monitor. Early life attachment experiences massively influence brain, neuronal, and pathway development, as well as bodily health.

The complex dissociative disorders, including DID and DDNOS, are entirely valid, demonstrable, extremely distressing conditions that are responsive to appropriate specialised treatments. The state of current NHS services may be understandable but it is no longer excusable.

References

Aquarone, R., & Hughes, W. (2005). The history of dissociation and trauma in the UK and its impact on treatment. *Journal of Trauma Practice, 4*: 305–322. DOI:10.1300/J189v04n03_07

Cantopher, T. (2007). *Stress-Related Illness*. London: Sheldon.

Cantopher, T. (2012). *Depressive Illness: the Curse of the Strong* (3rd edn). London: Sheldon.

Faulks, S. (2008). *Human Traces*. New York: Vintage.

Hatloy, I. (2013). *Understanding Dissociative Disorders*. London: Mind.

Hopper, J. W., Frewen, P. A., van der Kolk, B. A., Lanius, R. A. (2007). Neural correlates of re-experiencing, avoidance and dissociation in PTSD: symptom dimensions and emotion dysregulation in responses to script-driven trauma imagery. *Journal of Traumatic Stress, 20*: 713–725.

International Society for the Study of Trauma and Dissociation. (2011). Guidelines for treating dissociative identity disorder in adults, third revision. *Journal of Trauma and Dissociation, 12*: 2, 115–187.

Lloyd, M. (2011). How investing in therapeutic services provides a clinical cost saving long term. *Health Service Journal* (online), 1 September.

Ogden, P., Minton, K., & Pain, C. (2006). *Trauma and the Body: A Sensorimotor Approach to Psychotherapy*. New York: Norton.

Schore, A. N. (2003). *Affect Regulation and Disorders of the Self*. New York: Norton.
Sidran Traumatic Stress Institute (2010). What is a Dissociative Disorder? Online at: www.sidran.org/sub.cfm?contentID=75&sectionid=4
Steinberg, M., & Schnall, M. (2001). *The Stranger in the Mirror. Dissociation— the Hidden Epidemic*. New York: HarperCollins.

Other resources

European Society for Trauma and Dissociation: www.estd.org
First Person Plural: www.firstpersonplural.org.uk
Trauma and Abuse Group: www.tag-uk.net
Willows Counselling Service: www.willowscounselling.org.uk

CHAPTER TWELVE

How far have we come?

Orit Badouk Epstein

If you hear a voice within you say "you cannot paint" then by all means paint and that voice will be silenced.

—Vincent Van Gogh

A few years ago I visited the New National Gallery in Berlin. The exhibition at the time was called *Bilder Träume*, which means "picture dreams"—the theme was surrealism and the artists' dream paintings. Many of the great surrealist artists were represented, including Max Ernst, Salvador Dali, Joan Miró, Marcel Duchamp, Pablo Picasso, and Frida Kahlo. Only Kahlo resented being part of this group. She said: "They thought I was a surrealist but I wasn't, I never painted dreams. I painted my own reality. Really I do not know whether my paintings are surrealist or not, but I do know that they are a frankest expression of myself." (*Time* magazine 1953, Mexican autobiography)

This remarkable collection of writings is also a painting of a reality and the frankest expression of many selves. The authors are survivors of extreme trauma and ritual abuse, and their accounts tell of the experience of living with Dissociative Identity Disorder (DID). Some show the roots of these painful memories, sharing experiences that were denied by people around the authors but which, in order for them to survive, had to be stored and concealed in hidden pockets of existence. As we can read in this book, those memories persist.

Helping to organise the campaign day and being part of the creative process behind this book is a humbling experience. It is also a sign of the changes that are currently occurring with so many survivors who were once powerless and helpless children now being listened to and believed. I feel that we are in a similar process to that of the young child's development that Winnicott (1990) described. We are still in the early stages of relative dependency where "the infant's growth takes the form of a continuous interchange between inner and outer reality, each enriched by the other. The child is now not only a potential creator of the world but also the child becomes able to populate the world with samples of his or her own inner life." The narratives in this book eloquently express the dialogue between inner psychic history and external words. In listening, we allow the contributors to finally be believed and move towards autonomy and independence.

Kim Noble's sensitive account of her first exhibition as an artist with DID is reminiscent of Frida Kahlo's description of her own reality. In Chapter Two Kim describes her experience: "I remembered our first exhibition in London and the feeling of closeness, warmth and pride. I felt as I looked around the gallery it helped me realise for the first time that this was the nearest I was ever going to get to meeting my alters."

In Chapter Three, Nicky Robertson vividly describes that having DID is like "a whole necklace but it may be made up of any number of different colours and types of beads. The difference between someone with DID, and someone without, is the connections between the beads are not there. But all the beads are still needed to make the complete necklace that is the whole person."

In Chapter Four, Oriel Winslow beautifully reflects on the mirror images of the condition as it is perceived from the inside and outside and how this feels. "DID from the inside looks very different than from the outside—I was not aware of the switching because I literally wasn't there to witness it. With DID one has to have an inner creativity of self-care and compassion. Seeing it as internal family who can make democratic choices and good enough comprises."

In Chapter Five, Deborah Briggs and Carolyn Bramhall share their thoughts on the role of friendship. As each person with DID faces different sets of dilemmas, dependency on the therapist and separation anxiety can be helped with a safe friend or, as Deborah suggests, a safe network of friends whose help "dilutes the intensity of relationships when friends come to understand this bizarre behaviour. The relationships are renewed, the person with DID is no longer seen as the problem but as the hero."

Taking a common sense approach, Carolyn Bramhall says that "if the DID is presented in a factual and non-sensational manner, it is usually well received and believed". She concludes that some survivors have the inner resources to just have one friend, some need a group of friends, and some can't do without an intense relationship with a professional therapist. All people with DID, though, find life a hardship without a solid and safe attachment. The quality of the relationship can be healing and with friends, one can overcome the limitations of therapy and its constraining boundaries. A friend of Deborah's states that she can make creative adjustments in juggling the two roles without much fear: "A wise person once explained, as a therapist I am available to the client for the session but to a friend I would be very unlikely to give so much attention. The goal of therapy is healing and ending. The goal of friendship is healing and can be unending."

In Chapter Six, Paula Bennett gives a brave and moving account of dissociation as a survivor of satanic ritual abuse, describing how diagnosis changed her life. She says: "Survivors may be so scared to talk that they split into another person just to prevent the whole sordid truth from being remembered. At the clinic, I finally received the best present of all: a diagnosis of DID." Paula's determination, bravery, and gratitude to all the good people she's been helped by has enabled her to create a sense of safety and freedom from the cult and to be able to walk around without having to look over her shoulder.

In Chapter Seven, Carolyn Spring writes about our culture of denial. She astutely challenges the many aspects of denial surrounding DID: "Can I really be telling the truth when I talk of atrocities among the middle class? If we can't contemplate the reality of 100 days of genocide in Africa, we certainly must deny the reality of ritualised organised extreme abuse in Middle England." With the help of today's cyber technology, the web, Twitter and Facebook, Carolyn calls for a corporate telling and corporate assault on society's denial. The voice of truth is freely available to all survivors.

Chapter Eight is written by Caitlyn, one of Carol Broad's alters. Her tragic story is one where she realised that self-harm was no longer a defence against the horrendous abuse that she had received. She also realised how much her missing her children, because of her hospitalisation, affected her and made her end it. She acknowledges the help of a good friend who treated her multiplicity no differently, unlike many who seemed to think she had grown three heads. "It's a friendship we all hope and know will continue throughout the years to come, made in the darkest and desperate of times but that today brings great joy into our life." Carole's fight for funding and fight for recognition of being multiple feels like she has to climb Everest on a regular basis. Like Paula Bennett, Carole is ever so grateful for her diagnosis as a key to accessing funding and services. The acronym SHINE is an inspiring one too: We know from experience that with Support comes Hope and Inspiration for New beginnings with Endless possibilities.

In Chapter Nine, Rob Spring's love and patience is evident as he describes the pitfalls of being a partner of a DID survivor where, without previous experience of the condition, nothing could ever have prepared him for what was to happen in their relationship. Watching his wife turning "mad" at night had driven them to the edge. The impact this experience has had on his emotional state is clearly a case of the secondary re-traumatising we often witness that takes place with the unprepared and shocked relatives. In surviving the experiences he writes: "We started to heal our attachment breaches and I'm very glad that we did." The process that enabled Rob to stay in the relationship with Carolyn has also enabled them to create PODS—Positive Outcomes for Dissociative Survivors. In creating PODS, Rob and Carolyn have helped many survivors to hold on to hope and develop recovery plans.

Sue Bridger's account in Chapter Ten is rich in metaphors as she shares how to live well in the present, parenting oneself whilst mindful of inner children. Her toolkit is intended to keep her safe beyond her comfort zone. Sue's senses play a large part—the smell of hand cream, the touch of a smooth pebble, and a snack to eat—and she has taught herself how to parent her inner children at times of stress and anxiety. Dealing with DID needs a gentle approach, like opening a bottle of fizzy drink slowly to make sure it doesn't overflow. Sue has reassuring dialogues with her inner children and no longer sees her abuser. She writes: "Up till then, while contact was still taking place, it was a bit like driving a car with the brake and the accelerator pressed down at the same time. It takes courage but it's worth wearing this badge of authenticity as a part of my battle dress to touch on wholeness and truth in my being."

In Chapter Eleven, Dr Ruth Cureton clearly explains the validity of a DID diagnosis from a medical and scientific perspective. She convincingly portrays DID as a real response to life-threatening events and makes it hard to argue against the evidence. Ruth explains that "if a person is barely managing to stop themselves from drowning by holding on to a bit of flotsam, then what's needed is a non-judgemental context to consider a safe enough alternative 'lifeboat' before we can expect them to let the flotsam go. This myriad of symptoms and disorders mean that survivors face isolation, misunderstanding, and misdiagnosis."

In *For Your Own Good*, Alice Miller wrote: "When feelings are admitted into consciousness, the wall of silence disintegrates and the truth can no longer be held back." For decades survivors of ritual abuse were held back not only by their own silence and society's disbelief but also by multiple diagnoses of being mad, schizoid, borderline, and many more. This powerful collection bristling with creativity has enabled yet another important leap to occur, integrating the reality of the children who once endured so much abuse and acknowledging the validity of DID after so much misdiagnosis. By acknowledging the DID diagnosis we as a society can no longer escape from believing the shocking reality that atrocities and crimes against powerless children exist in our so-called civilised society.

Rather than classifying it as a disorder, DID is a normative response to overwhelming experiences such as torture and abuse. We know DID symptoms lead to a lack of coherence and coordination within the survivor's personality as a whole. As a psychotherapist I often hear clients describing DID as being like getting lost in the head to avoid remembering the unremembered, forgetting the unforgettable, and shutting down their internal cries.

Tomkins wrote that affect is the psychic glue that holds the experience of the self together (Monsen & Monsen, 1999). Like the metaphor of the necklace described in Chapter Three, the thread of continuity between all the chapters in this book successfully enables a cohesive and coherent narrative to emerge. This, I am sure, will help fragmented others to glue their truth together and come forward, as this truth can no longer be ignored, denied, or covered up.

References

Miller, A. (1985). *For Your Own Good*. New York: Farrar Straus and Giroux.
Winnicott, D. W. (1990). *The Maturational Processes and the Facilitating Environment*. London: Karnac.

INDEX

1 Corinthians 20
2 Corinthians 68

abortion 18–19, 55
acceptance 101
acute stress reaction 117
addiction 110, 112
adrenaline 96
Afghan War 113
Africa 63
AIDS 59
alchemy 2
All of Me (Kim Noble) xi, 4
alters 67
    friends feel out of their depth
        over 43–44
    grief over loss of 5
    handwriting 33, 76
    host and 32
    individual quirks 76
    information provided by 4
    integrating other alters 87
    meeting 6
    mood swings 76
    new ones present themselves 37
    numbers of vary 67
    painting by 6–11
    PTSD and 73
    putting on hold 31
    terror in 30
    traumatised 28
    university life and 24–26
Am I A Good Girl Yet? (Carolyn
    Bramhall) ix
American Psychiatric Association 89
amnesia 112
amygdala 108–109
anger 84
anorexia 25
anxiety 108, 110
Aquarone & Hughes 113
atrocities 58–59, 125

attachment
    Bowlby Centre 1
    disorders 114
    disorganised 106–108, 112
    friends and 38
    life hard without 125
    lifelong effect of issues
        concerning 120
    theory and issues 14
    therapist's role 36
Attachment xi
awareness 64

Baby P 60, 63
Bamber, Helen 65
Bangladesh 63
behavioural strategies, list of 110
Bennett, Paula ix, 49–56, 125–126
benzodiazepine 68
Bible
    1 Corinthians 20
    2 Corinthians 68
    creation and a creator 15
    New Testament 78
    out of the kingdom of
        darkness 16
Bilder Träume (New National Gallery,
        Berlin) 123
bipolar disorder 15
Black Mass 50
blame 74, 84
body, the
    brain and 118
    coping strategies 4
    DID patients and 3
    memories 76, 96
    mind and 13, 105, 119
    St Paul describes 20
boundaries 35, 38, 41, 45
Bowlby, John ix, 60
Bowlby, Richard ix
Bowlby, Xenia ix, xiii–xiv

Bowlby Centre 1
brain, the 118
brain stem 108
Bramhall, Carolyn ix, 35–47,
        124–125
breathing 95
Bridger, Sue x, 93–103, 126
Briggs, Deborah x, 35–47, 124–125
British Empire 63
British Psychological Society xi
Broad, Carol x, 67–79, 125–126
Burke, Edmund 40

campaign days xiii, 3, 124
campaigning 64
Cantopher, Dr Tim 105
Carlile, Tina 2
child abuse *see also* ritual abuse;
        satanic ritual abuse
    as murder of the soul 14
    case study of denial 57–60
    daily ordeal of 52
    dangers of discussing with
        friends 88
    extreme and organised 87, 107
    paintings 9
    repeated and overwhelming 85
    severe long-term consequences
        of 113
child pornography 87–88
childhood trauma 77, 93, 106 *see also*
        trauma
children, victimisation of 39
choice 17
Christianity x, 14, 17–21, 39
church services 21
Clarkson, Thomas 64
climate change 59
Clinic for Dissociative Studies (CDS)
        x, 1, 54
cognition 109
Cohen, Leonard 100

Colossians 16
comfort zones 94
commitments 97
communication books 3
communion 21, 52
community, need for 47
co-morbidities 110, 112
computer coding 115–118
Connelly, Peter 60, 63
coping mechanisms
    complex nature of 4
    drastic solutions 111
    friends and 46
    overwhelmed 107
    self harm as 86
    widely misunderstood 110
Corinthians 20, 68
cortex 108–109
cortisol 108
courage 47
covens 49–51, 55
creation 15
Cureton, Dr Ruth x, 105–121, 127

deadlines 29
definition (DID) 89
denial 57–65, 88, 125
Department of Health 59
depression 15–16, 18, 37
diagnosis
    best present of all 54
    changing ones life through 125
    Clinic for Dissociative Studies 1
    computer coding lists of 115–118
    funding and professional
        scepticism 75
    journey to, a 51
    key to accessing services 78
    misdiagnosis 113–114, 127
    multiple 127
    NHS and 79
    notion of 29

tests and investigations 105
treatment time from 106
dissociation
    accepting 101
    culture of denial around 59
    denial and 62
    depicting on canvas 9
    describing 58, 89, 107–108
    dynamics of 40–41
    main tool of separation 51
Dissociative Disorder Not Otherwise
        Specified (DDNOS) 107, 112,
        118, 120
dissociative disorders, classification
        of 115–117
doctors 60, 77, 105
dreams 123
drinking 5
DSM-IV 75, 118
DSM-5 (Diagnostic and Statistical
        Manual of Mental Disorders,
        fifth edition) 115
duplicates (of possessions) 76

East Anglia 63
eating disorders 26, 28, 112
Epstein, Orit Badouk x, 4, 123–128
Equiano, Olaudah 64
European Society for Trauma and
        Dissociation (ESTD) x–xi

Facebook 58
fake culture 58
Falklands War 113
Faulks, Sebastian 119
feelings 99–100
fight, flight or freeze 107, 109
First Person Plural (FPP) x, xii
flashbacks
    absolute terror of 83
    intrusiveness of 28–29, 109
    under siege from 96

For Your Own Good (Alice Miller) 127
forgetfulness 76
forgiveness 17
Frankish, Dr Pat xi, 1–4
Freud, Sigmund 119
friends 35–47
    coming between husband and
        wife 84
    driven away 61–62
    growing apart from 88
    judging for who you are 74
    on their own or a network
        124–125
    suitability of 99–100
funding 75, 77–79, 114, 126

genocide 58
God
    as best lifeline 56
    as creator 15
    considering the existence of 17
    New Testament words 78
    spiritual journey towards 19–20
    taking your punishment for you
        16
good and evil 14–15, 17
Gray Healthcare 77
Ground Zero 58
guilt 16, 18, 50, 74

Halloween 49
Hatloy, I. 107
healing
    acceptance and 101
    friendship and 45
    goal of therapy 45, 125
    no fixed path 36
    not an easy process 90
    quality of friendship and 44
    YouTube video 96
Health Service Journal 106
Heart for Truth ix, 38

Herman, Judith Lewis 59
hippocampus 109, 119–120
holistic approaches 113
Holocaust 59
hopelessness, sense of 39
hospitals 71–74 106
Human Traces (Sebastian Faulks) 119
hyperarousal 109

ICD-10 (International Classification
    of Diseases, 10th revision)
    115–116, 118
incest 49, 64, 88, 108
insomnia 76
Institute of Psychotherapy and
    Disability xi
Interact (TAG) xii
"internal chaos" 76
internal group dynamics 31

Janet, Pierre 119
Jesus Christ 16, 20
Jews 59

Kabbalah 9
Kahlo, Frida 123–124
King, Pearl 2
Kübler-Ross, Elisabeth 59

Lantern Project 60
limbic system 108
Lloyd, M. 106, 111–112

Manchester United 86
memories
    as infestation 57
    critical period of surfacing 37
    dark corridors of 38
    doubting 62
    lack of re alters 5–6
    of the body 76, 96
    storage of 108–109, 119

triggering 41
working through 42, 45
Mental Health Acts 73, 75
mental health services 113
migrants 63
Miller, Alice 127
mind, the 13, 47, 105, 119
mind control 15, 43
Ministry of Justice 73
Monsen & Monsen 127
mood swings 76, 108
moral standards 14
MRI scans 107, 119–120
Multiple Parts (PODS) xii, 90

narratives 29, 62–63, 87, 124
National Institute for Health and
    Care Excellence (NICE) 115
nervous system 107–108
neuroscience 119
New National Gallery, Berlin 123
New Testament 78
NHS
    acute psychiatric wards 74
    adults equally deserving of
        treatment 112
    diagnosis difficulties 79
    investment in therapy and
        106
    postcode lotteries within
        75, 79
    surviving within x
    understandable but not
        excusable 120
"no further action" 62
Noble, Kim xi, 4–11, 124

Obholzer, Anton 3
objects 102
Observer 2
Ogden, Minton & Pain 109
orphans, Romanian 107

pain 47, 64, 72
painting (by alters) 5–11
Paracelsus 2
Paracelsus Trust
    Deborah Briggs x
    independence of 3
    Pat Frankish xi, 2
    Xenia Bowlby ix
parent figures 107
parenting 31 *see also* re-parenting
partial solutions 110
Paul, St. 20
Peak District 15
Pentecostalism x
Peter Pan (J. M. Barrie) 27
pets 94
PODS (Positive Outcomes for
        Dissociative Survivors)
        xi–xii, 90–91, 126
police 89
possessions 102
postcode lotteries 75, 79
postgraduates 28
post-traumatic stress disorder
        (PTSD)
    core symptoms 117–118
    issues within 112
    neglect of attachment needs and
        107
    secure environment for sufferer
        73
    wartime examples 113
Power of Now, The (Eckhart Tolle) 95
Priory, The 74
psychiatric wards 71
psychotherapy 62, 106 *see also*
        therapy
punishment 16–17, 50

rape 64, 88
Read Codes 115
reassurance 98–99

re-parenting 95, 98 *see also* parenting
ritual abuse *see also* child abuse;
        satanic ritual abuse
    a main cause 1
    continuing concern over 37
    core identity attacked by 2
    explaining to others 40–41
    multiple incorrect diagnoses 127
    systems produced by 3
    training friends to help survivors
        39
Ritual Abuse and Mind Control: The
    Manipulation of Attachment
    Needs (Orik Badouk Epstein
    and others) x–xi
rituals 17
Roberts, Amelia 3
Robertson, Nicky xi, 13–21, 124
Romanian orphans 107
Rothschild, Babette 96
Royal Holloway xii
Rumi the mystic 100
Rwanda 58

sacrifice 16–17
safe places 94, 102
safety 39
Sanderson, C. 60
satanic ritual abuse (SRA) 49–56 *see*
        also child abuse; ritual abuse
    Am I A Good Girl Yet? ix
    bringing into the open 41
    Christian values inverted by 21
    holding a faith and 13
    non-professionals' involvement
        43
satanism 15, 21
Savile, Jimmy ix
Schofield, Philip xi
SCID-D (Structured Clinical
        Interview for DSM-IV
        Dissociative Disorders) 75

secondary traumatic stress 88
secrecy 37, 61–62, 65
self-harming
    a husband discovers 83
    as coping mechanism 86
    equated with attention seeking
        72
    growing worse 71
    on hospital wards 74
    seeming the best option 101–102
self worth 14–15
separation anxiety 36
sexual abuse 60 *see also* child abuse;
        ritual abuse; satanic ritual
        abuse
shame 16, 61, 74, 111–112
SHINE 79, 126
Shipman, Harold 60, 63
Sidran Institute 106
Sidran Traumatic Stress Foundation
        106
silence 62
Sinason, Valerie 1
slave trade 63–65
sleep 76
sleep walking 5–6
smoking 59
SNOMED CT (Systematized
        Nomenclature of Medicine-
        Clinical Terms) 115
Snow Queen (Hans Christian
        Andersen) 27
social services 8
solitude 94–95
soul 14–15
specialists 113
spiritual journeys 20–21
spiritual trauma 6, 13–21
splitting 4, 28, 50
Spring, Carolyn xi, 57–66, 81–91,
        125–126
Spring, Rob 81–91, 126

START (Survivors Trauma and
        Abuse Recovery Trust) xii
Steinberg & Schnall 106
stigma 111
stress, post-traumatic 107 *see also*
        Post-Traumatic Stress
        Disorder (PTSD)
students xi, 23 *see also* university life
sugar trade 63
suicide 15, 43, 72
Sunday Express ix
superiority, feelings of 44
surrealism 123
survival mechanisms and responses
        1, 19, 107–108
survivors
    assessment and treatment
        required for 114
    awareness of evil 14
    campaign days 3
    crises out of office hours 46
    crisis points 106
    detachment 58
    DID and 4, 19
    failures suffered by 79
    friends and family 37
    friendship teams 39, 42, 47
    from problem to hero 41
    groups ix
    growth of survivor movement 37
    "lone rangers" 38
    non-professional help, does it
        work? 43, 46
    patronising attitudes towards 44
    PODS xii
    possible range of difficulties
        facing 112
    practical needs 42
    re-traumatising experiences 119
    satanic rituals, of 21
    scared to talk 125
    secrecy of 37

spiritual aspect 21
splitting as defence mechanism
        50
START xii
    tips from a 102–103
    university, at 27
    wary of disclosure 35
Swansea University xii
switching 4, 24, 76, 124
symptoms, list of 110
systems 3

TAG (Trauma and Abuse Group)
        x, xii
TASC (Trauma and Abuse Support
        Centre) xi, 90
terror 30, 82–85, 87
therapists
    advice to 97–98
    dealing with information from
        alters 4
    dependence on 36
    keeping functioning parts
        functioning 26
    professional boundaries 35, 45, 88
    recognising trauma as root cause
        28
    talking to about host and alters
        32
    toolkits for x
    TOP DD study 106
therapy *see also* psychotherapy
    early experiences of 53
    goal of 45, 125
    hippocampus during 120
    investing in 106
    relationship with therapist 97–98
This Morning xi
Thompson, Emma 65
thyroid gland disorders 118
Time magazine 123
tips (from a surviver) 102–103

Tolle, Eckhart 95
Tomkins, Silvan 127
toolkits x, 95, 126
torture 65, 88, 127
Towson University, Maryland 106
training, medical 114–115
training, of friends 39–40
trauma
    acceptance of childhood trauma
        77
    denial as response to 59, 63
    disorganised attachment and 107
    dissociation brought on by 107
    flashbacks and 109
    hippocampus and 120
    journey from childhood trauma
        93
    long term consequences 106, 113
    recovery 40, 114
    retraumatising by health
        professionals 119
    secondary stress 88
    slow healing 96
    spiritual 6, 13–21
    therapist recognises 28
    whole system impact of 120
Trauma and Abuse Group (TAG)
        x, xii
treatment
    appreciation of 111
    budget deficit and 62
    Clinic for Dissociative Studies 1
    computer coding 115
    having to fight for 79

lack of options 63
lack of specialist services 75
refusal of funding 114
timescale from diagnosis 106
Treatment of Patients with
        Dissociative Disorders, The
        (TOP DD) 106
triggering 109
triune brain 108

university life 23–30, 32–33

Van Gogh, Vincent 123
victimisation 39
violence 30
vulnerability 100

wars 113
wealth 58
Wedgwood, Josiah 64
West Indies 63
Wilberforce, William 63–65
Willoughby, Holly xi
Willows Counselling Service,
        Swindon x
"windows of tolerance" 94, 109
Winfrey, Oprah xi
Winnicott, Donald 124
Winslow, Oriel xii, 23–33, 124
witchcraft 49
World War I 113
World War II 113

YouTube video 96